The LSAT® Explained...

The Official LSAT PrepTest

With Explanations™

Volume One

A Publication of the Law School Admission Council

The Law School Admission Council is a nonprofit corporation that provides services to the legal education community. Its members are 197 law schools in the United States and Canada.

LSAT®; *The Official LSAT PrepTest*®; *LSAT: The Official TriplePrep*®; and the Law Services logo are registered marks of the Law School Admission Council, Inc. Law School Forum is a service mark of the Law School Admission Council, Inc. *LSAT: The Official TriplePrep Plus; The Official LSAT PrepTest With Explanations; The Whole Law School Package; The Official Guide to U.S. Law Schools*; and *LSACD* are trademarks of the Law School Admission Council, Inc.

Law School Admission Council fees, policies, and procedures relating to, but not limited to, test registration, test administration, test score reporting, misconduct and irregularities, and other matters may change without notice at any time. To remain up-to-date on Law School Admission Council policies and procedures, you may obtain a current *LSAT/LSDAS Registration and Information Book*, or you may contact our candidate service representatives.

ISBN 0-942639-68-5

Table of Contents

The Law School Admission Test is a half-day standardized test required for admission to all 197 LSAC-member law schools. It consists of five 35-minute sections of multiple-choice questions. Four of the five sections contribute to the test taker's score. These sections include one reading comprehension section, one analytical reasoning section, and two logical reasoning sections. The unscored section typically is used to pretest new test items and to preequate new test forms. A 30-minute writing sample is administered at the end of the test. The writing sample is not scored by LSAC; however, copies of the writing sample are sent to all law schools to which you apply. The score scale for the LSAT is 120 to 180, with 120 being the lowest possible score and 180 the highest possible score.

The LSAT is designed to measure skills that are considered essential for success in law school: the reading and comprehension of complex texts with accuracy and insight; the organization and management of information and the ability to draw reasonable inferences from it; the ability to think critically; and the analysis and evaluation of the reasoning and arguments of others.

The LSAT provides a standard measure of acquired reading and verbal reasoning skills that law schools can use as one of several factors in assessing applicants.

Scoring

Your LSAT score is based on the number of questions you answer correctly (the raw score). There is no deduction for incorrect answers, and all questions count equally. In other words, there is no penalty for guessing.

■ Test Score Accuracy—Reliability and Standard Error of Measurement

Candidates perform at different levels on different occasions for reasons quite unrelated to the characteristics of a test itself. The accuracy of test scores is best described by the use of two related statistical terms, reliability and standard error of measurement.

Reliability is a measure of how consistently a test measures the skills being assessed. The higher the reliability coefficient for a test, the more certain we can be that test takers would get very similar scores if they took the test again.

LSAC reports an internal consistency measure of reliability for every test form. Reliability can vary from 0.00 to 1.00, and a test with no measurement error would have a reliability coefficient of 1.00 (never attained in practice). Reliability coefficients for past LSAT forms have ranged from .90 to .95, indicating a high degree of consistency for these tests. LSAC expects the reliability of the LSAT to continue to fall within the same range.

LSAC also reports the amount of measurement error associated with each test form, a concept known as the standard error of measurement (SEM). The SEM, which is usually about 2.6 points, indicates how close a test

taker's observed score is likely to be to his or her true score. True scores are hypothetical scores that are only obtainable from perfectly reliable tests with no measurement error—scores never known in practice.

Score bands, or ranges of scores that contain a test taker's true score a certain percentage of the time, can be derived using the SEM. LSAT score bands are constructed by adding and subtracting the (rounded) SEM to and from an actual LSAT score (e.g., the LSAT score, plus or minus 3 points). Scores near 120 or 180 have asymmetrical bands. Score bands constructed in this manner will contain an individual's true score approximately 68 percent of the time.

Measurement error also must be taken into account when comparing LSAT scores of two test takers. It is likely that small differences in scores are due to measurement error rather than to meaningful differences in ability. The standard error of score differences provides some guidance as to the importance of differences between two scores. The standard error of score differences is approximately 1.4 times larger than the standard error of measurement for the individual scores.

Thus, a test score should be regarded as a useful but approximate measure of a test taker's abilities as measured by the test, not as an exact determination of his or her abilities. LSAC encourages law schools to examine the range of scores within the interval that probably contains the test taker's true score (e.g., the test taker's score band) rather than solely interpret the reported score alone.

■ Adjustments for Variation in Test Difficulty

All test forms of the LSAT reported on the same score scale are designed to measure the same abilities, but one test form may be slightly easier or more difficult than another. The scores from different test forms are made comparable through a statistical procedure known as equating. As a result of equating, a given scaled score earned on different test forms reflects the same level of ability.

■ Research on the LSAT

Summaries of LSAT validity studies and other LSAT research can be found in member law school libraries.

How This PrepTest Differs From an Actual LSAT

This PrepTest is made up of the scored sections and writing sample from an actual LSAT. However, it does not contain the extra, variable section that is used to pretest new test items of one of the three question types. Also, you are likely to encounter the three LSAT question types in a different order when you take an actual LSAT than they are in this PrepTest. This is because the order of the question types is intentionally varied for each administration of the test.

The Question Types

The multiple-choice questions that make up most of the LSAT reflect a broad range of academic disciplines and are intended to give no advantage to candidates from a particular academic background.

The five sections of the test contain three different question types. The following material presents a general discussion of the nature of each question type and some strategies that can be used in answering them.

■ Logical Reasoning Questions

Logical reasoning questions evaluate a test taker's ability to understand, analyze, criticize, and complete arguments. The arguments are contained in short passages taken from a variety of sources, including letters to the editor, speeches, advertisements, newspaper articles and editorials, informal discussions and conversations, as well as articles in the humanities, the social sciences, and the natural sciences.

Each logical reasoning question requires the examinee to read and comprehend the argument or the reasoning contained in the passage, and answer one or two questions about it. The questions test a variety of logical skills. These include:

- recognizing the point or issue of an argument or dispute;

- detecting the assumptions involved in an argumentation or chain of reasoning;

- drawing reasonable conclusions from given evidence or premises;

- identifying and applying principles;

- identifying the method or structure of an argument or chain of reasoning;

- detecting reasoning errors and misinterpretations;

- determining how additional evidence or argumentation affects an argument or conclusion; and

- identifying explanations and recognizing resolutions of conflicting facts or arguments.

The questions do not presuppose knowledge of the terminology of formal logic. For example, you will not be expected to know the meaning of specialized terms such as "ad hominem" or "syllogism." On the other hand, you will be expected to understand and critique the reasoning contained in arguments. This requires that you possess, at a minimum, a college-level understanding of widely used concepts such as argument, premise, assumption, and conclusion.

Suggested Approach

Read each question carefully. Make sure that you understand the meaning of each part of the question. Make sure that you understand the meaning of each answer choice and the ways in which it may or may not relate to the question posed.

Do not pick a response simply because it is a true statement. Although true, it may not answer the question posed.

Answer each question on the basis of the information that is given, even if you do not agree with it. Work within the context provided by the passage. LSAT questions do not involve any tricks or hidden meanings.

■ Reading Comprehension Questions

The purpose of reading comprehension questions is to measure your ability to read, with understanding and insight, examples of lengthy and complex materials similar to those commonly encountered in law school work. The reading comprehension section of the test consists of four passages, each approximately 450 words long, followed by five to eight questions that test your reading and reasoning abilities. Passages for reading comprehension items draw from subjects such as the humanities, the social sciences, biological and physical sciences, and issues related to the law.

Reading comprehension questions require test takers to read carefully and accurately, to determine the relationships among the various parts of the passage, and to draw reasonable inferences from the material in the passage. The questions may ask about:

- the main idea or primary purpose of the passage;

- the meaning or purpose of words or phrases used in the passage;

- information explicitly stated in the passage;

- information or ideas that can be inferred from the passage;

- the organization of the passage;

- the application of information in the passage to a new context; and

- the tone of the passage or the author's attitude as it is revealed in the language used.

Suggested Approach

Since passages are drawn from many different disciplines and sources, you should not be discouraged if you encounter material with which you are not familiar. It is important to remember that questions are to be answered exclusively on the basis of the information provided in the passage. There is no particular knowledge that you are expected to bring to the test, and you should not make inferences based on any prior knowledge of a subject that you may have. You may, however, wish to defer working on a passage that seems particularly difficult or unfamiliar until after you have dealt with passages you find easier.

Strategies. In preparing for the test, you should experiment with different strategies, and decide which work most effectively for you. These include:

- Reading the passage very closely and then answering the questions;

- Reading the questions first, reading the passage closely, and then returning to the questions; and

- Skimming the passage and questions very quickly, then rereading the passage closely and answering the questions.

Remember that your strategy must be effective under timed conditions.

Reading the passage. Whatever strategy you choose, you should give the passage at least one careful reading before answering the questions. Separate main ideas from supporting ideas and the author's own ideas or attitudes from factual, objective information. Note transitions from one idea to the next and examine the relationships among the different ideas or parts of the passage. For example, are they contrasting or complementary? Consider how and why the author makes points and draws conclusions. Be sensitive to the implications of what the passage says.

You may find it helpful to mark key parts of the passage. For example, you might underline main ideas or important arguments, and you might circle transitional words—'although,' 'nevertheless,' 'correspondingly,' and the like—that will help you map the structure of the passage. Moreover, you might note descriptive words that will help you identify the author's attitude toward a particular idea or person.

Answering the Questions

- Always read all the answer choices before selecting the best answer. The best answer choice is the one that most accurately and completely answers the question being posed.

- Respond to the specific question being asked. Do not pick an answer choice simply because it is a true statement. For example, picking a true statement might yield an incorrect answer to a question in which you are asked to identify the author's position on an issue, since here you are not being asked to evaluate the truth of the author's position, but only to correctly identify what that position is.

- Answer the questions only on the basis of the information provided in the passage. Your own views, interpretations, or opinions, and those you have heard from others, may sometimes conflict with those expressed in the passage; however, you are expected to work within the context provided by the passage. You should not expect to agree with everything you encounter in reading comprehension passages.

■ Analytical Reasoning Questions

Analytical reasoning items are designed to measure the ability to understand a structure of relationships and to draw conclusions about the structure. The examinee is asked to make deductions from a set of statements, rules, or conditions that describe relationships among entities such as persons, places, things, or events. They simulate the kinds of detailed analyses of relationships that a law student must perform in solving legal problems. For example, a passage might describe four diplomats sitting around a table, following certain rules of protocol as to who can sit where. The test taker must answer questions about the implications of the given information, for example, who is sitting between diplomats X and Y.

The passage used for each group of questions describes a common relationship such as the following:

- Assignment: Two parents, P and O, and their children, R and S, must go to the dentist on four consecutive days, designated 1, 2, 3, and 4;

- Ordering: X arrived before Y but after Z;

- Grouping: A manager is trying to form a project team from seven staff members—R,S,T,U,V,W, and X. Each staff member has a particular strength—writing, planning, or facilitating;

- Spatial: A certain country contains six cities and each city is connected to at least one other city by a system of roads, some of which are one-way.

Careful reading and analysis are necessary to determine the exact nature of the relationships involved. Some relationships are fixed (e.g., P and R always sit at the same table). Other relationships are variable (e.g., Q must be assigned to either table 1 or table 3). Some relationships that are not stated in the conditions are implied by and can be deduced from those that are stated. (e.g., If one condition about books on a shelf specifies that Book L is to the left of Book Y, and another specifies that Book P is to the left of Book L, then it can be deduced that Book P is to the left of Book Y.) No formal training in logic is required to answer these questions correctly. Analytical reasoning questions are

intended to be answered using knowledge, skills, and reasoning ability generally expected of college students and graduates.

Suggested Approach

Some people may prefer to answer first those questions about a passage that seem less difficult and then those that seem more difficult. In general, it is best not to start another passage before finishing one begun earlier, because much time can be lost in returning to a passage and reestablishing familiarity with its relationships. Do not assume that, because the conditions for a set of questions look long or complicated, the questions based on those conditions will necessarily be especially difficult.

Reading the passage. In reading the conditions, do not introduce unwarranted assumptions. For instance, in a set establishing relationships of height and weight among the members of a team, do not assume that a person who is taller than another person must weigh more than that person. All the information needed to answer each question is provided in the passage and the question itself.

The conditions are designed to be as clear as possible; do not interpret them as if they were intended to trick you. For example, if a question asks how many people could be eligible to serve on a committee, consider only those people named in the passage unless directed otherwise. When in doubt, read the conditions in their most obvious sense. Remember, however, that the language in the conditions is intended to be read for precise meaning. It is essential to pay particular attention to words that describe or limit relationships, such as 'only,' 'exactly,' 'never,' 'always,' 'must be,' 'cannot be,' and the like.

The result of this careful reading will be a clear picture of the structure of the relationships involved, including the kinds of relationships permitted, the participants in the relationships, and the range of actions or attributes allowed by the relationships for these participants.

Questions are independent. Each question should be considered separately from the other questions in its set; no information, except what is given in the original conditions, should be carried over from one question to another. In some cases a question will simply ask for conclusions to be drawn from the conditions as originally given. Some questions may, however, add information to the original conditions or temporarily suspend one of the original conditions for the purpose of that question only. For example, if Question 1 adds the information "if P is sitting at table 2...," this information should NOT be carried over to any other question in the group.

Highlighting the text; using diagrams. Many people find it useful to underline key points in the passage and in each question. In addition, it may prove very helpful to draw a diagram to assist you in finding the solution to the problem.

In preparing for the test, you may wish to experiment with different types of diagrams. For a scheduling problem, a calendar-like diagram may be helpful. For a spatial relationship problem, a simple map can be a useful device.

Even though some people find diagrams to be very helpful, other people seldom use them. And among those who do regularly use diagrams in solving these problems, there is by no means universal agreement on which kind of diagram is best for which problem or in which cases a diagram is most useful. Do not be concerned if a particular problem in the test seems to be best approached without the use of a diagram.

The Writing Exercise

Test takers are given 30 minutes to complete the brief writing exercise, which is not scored but is used by law school admission personnel to assess writing skill. Read the topic carefully. You will probably find it best to spend a few minutes considering the topic and organizing your thoughts before you begin writing. **Do not write on a topic other than the one specified. Writing on a topic of your own choice is not acceptable.**

There is no "right" or "wrong" position on the writing sample topic. Law schools are interested in how skillfully you support the position you take and how clearly you express that position. How well you write is much more important than how much you write. No special knowledge is required or expected. Law schools are interested in organization, vocabulary, and writing mechanics. They understand the short time available to you and the pressure under which you are writing.

Confine your writing to the lined area following the writing sample topic. You will find that you have enough space if you plan your writing carefully, write on every line, avoid wide margins, and keep your handwriting a reasonable size. Be sure that your handwriting is legible.

Scratch paper is provided for use during the writing sample portion of the test only. Scratch paper cannot be used in other sections of the LSAT.

The writing sample is photocopied and sent to law schools to which you direct your LSAT score. A pen will be provided at the test center, which must be used (for the writing sample only) to ensure a photocopy of high quality.

Some writing sample prompts, or variations of them, may be given at more than one LSAT administration. A collection of 50 representative writing prompts is included in *LSAT: The Official TriplePrep Plus*, published by LSAC.

Taking the PrepTest Under Simulated LSAT Conditions

One important way to prepare for the LSAT is to take a sample test under the same requirements and time limits you will encounter in taking an actual LSAT. This helps you to estimate the amount of time you can afford to spend on each question in a section and to determine the question types on which you may need additional practice.

Since the LSAT is a timed test, it is important to use your allotted time wisely. During the test, you may work only on the section designated by the test supervisor. You cannot devote extra time to a difficult section and make up that time on a section you find easier. In pacing yourself, and checking your answers, you should think of each section of the test as a separate minitest.

Be sure that you answer every question on the test. When you do not know the correct answer to a question, first eliminate the responses that you know are incorrect, then make your best guess among the remaining choices. Do not be afraid to guess as there is no penalty for incorrect answers.

When you take a sample test abide by all the requirements specified in the directions and keep strictly within the specified time limits. Work without a rest period. When you take an actual test you will have only a short break—usually 10-15 minutes—after SECTION III. When taken under conditions as much like actual testing conditions as possible, a sample test provides very useful preparation for taking the LSAT.

Official directions for the four multiple-choice sections and the writing sample are included in this PrepTest so that you can approximate actual testing conditions as you practice.

To take the test:

- Set a timer for 35 minutes. Answer all the questions in SECTION I of this PrepTest. Stop working on that section when the 35 minutes have elapsed.

- Repeat, allowing yourself 35 minutes each for sections II, III, and IV.

- Set the timer for 30 minutes, then prepare your response to the writing sample for the PrepTest.

- Refer to "Computing Your Score" for the PrepTest for instruction on evaluating your performance. An answer key is provided for that purpose.

The sample test that follows consists of four sections corresponding to the four scored sections of the actual LSAT.

General Directions for the LSAT Answer Sheet

The actual testing time for this portion of the test will be 2 hours 55 minutes. There are five sections, each with a time limit of 35 minutes. The supervisor will tell you when to begin and end each section. If you finish a section before time is called, you may check your work on that section only; do not turn to any other section of the test book and do not work on any other section either in the test book or on the answer sheet.

There are several different types of questions on the test, and each question type has its own directions. Be sure you understand the directions for each question type before attempting to answer any questions in that section.

Not everyone will finish all the questions in the time allowed. Do not hurry, but work steadily and as quickly as you can without sacrificing accuracy. You are advised to use your time effectively. If a question seems too difficult, go on to the next one and return to the difficult question after completing the section. MARK THE BEST ANSWER YOU CAN FOR EVERY QUESTION. NO DEDUCTIONS WILL BE MADE FOR WRONG ANSWERS. YOUR SCORE WILL BE BASED ONLY ON THE NUMBER OF QUESTIONS YOU ANSWER CORRECTLY.

ALL YOUR ANSWERS MUST BE MARKED ON THE ANSWER SHEET. Answer spaces for each question are lettered to correspond with the letters of the potential answers to each question in the test book. After you have decided which of the answers is correct, blacken the corresponding space on the answer sheet. BE SURE THAT EACH MARK IS BLACK AND COMPLETELY FILLS THE ANSWER SPACE. Give only one answer to each question. If you change an answer, be sure that all previous marks are erased completely. Since the answer sheet is machine scored, incomplete erasures may be interpreted as intended answers. ANSWERS RECORDED IN THE TEST BOOK WILL NOT BE SCORED.

There may be more questions noted on this answer sheet than there are questions in a section. Do not be concerned but be certain that the section and number of the question you are answering matches the answer sheet section and question number. Additional answer spaces in any answer sheet section should be left blank. Begin your next section in the number one answer space for that section.

Law Services takes various steps to ensure that answer sheets are returned from test centers in a timely manner for processing. In the unlikely event that an answer sheet(s) is not received, Law Services will permit the examinee to either retest at no additional fee or to receive a refund of his or her LSAT fee. THESE REMEDIES ARE THE EXCLUSIVE REMEDIES AVAILABLE IN THE UNLIKELY EVENT THAT AN ANSWER SHEET IS NOT RECEIVED BY LAW SERVICES.

Score Cancellation

Complete this section only if you are absolutely certain you want to cancel your score. A CANCELLATION REQUEST CANNOT BE RESCINDED. IF YOU ARE AT ALL UNCERTAIN, YOU SHOULD NOT COMPLETE THIS SECTION; INSTEAD, YOU SHOULD USE THE TIME ALLOWED AFTER THE TEST (UP TO 5 DAYS) TO FULLY CONSIDER YOUR DECISION.

To cancel your score from this administration, you must:

A. fill in the ovals here........ ○ ○

B. read the following statement. Then sign your name and enter the date. YOUR SIGNATURE ALONE IS NOT SUFFICIENT FOR SCORE CANCELLATION. BOTH OVALS ABOVE MUST BE FILLED IN FOR SCANNING EQUIPMENT TO RECOGNIZE YOUR REQUEST FOR SCORE CANCELLATION.

I certify that I wish to cancel my test score from this administration. I understand that my request is irreversible and that my score will not be sent to me or to the law schools to which I apply.

_____
Sign your name in full

_____
Date

HOW DID YOU PREPARE FOR THE LSAT?
(Select all that apply.)

Responses to this item are voluntary and will be used for statistical research purposes only.

○ By studying the sample questions in the *LSAT Registration and Information Book*.
○ By taking the free sample LSAT in the *LSAT Registration and Information Book*.
○ By working through *The Official LSAT PrepTest(s), TriplePrep*.
○ By using a book on how to prepare for the LSAT not published by Law Services.
○ By attending a commercial test preparation or coaching course.
○ By attending a test preparation or coaching course offered through an undergraduate institution.
○ Self study.
○ Other preparation.
○ No preparation.

CERTIFYING STATEMENT

Please write (DO NOT PRINT) the following statement. Sign and date.

I certify that I am the examinee whose name appears on this answer sheet and that I am here to take the LSAT for the sole purpose of being considered for admission to law school. I further certify that I will neither assist nor receive assistance from any other candidate, and I agree not to copy or retain examination questions or to transmit them in any form to any other person.

_____
_____
_____
_____
_____
_____
_____
_____
_____

SIGNATURE: _____   TODAY'S DATE: ___/___/___
                                                                MONTH DAY YEAR

INSTRUCTIONS FOR COMPLETING THE BIOGRAPHICAL AREA ARE ON THE BACK COVER OF YOUR TEST BOOKLET.
USE ONLY A NO. 2 OR HB PENCIL TO COMPLETE THIS ANSWER SHEET. DO NOT USE INK.

1 LAST NAME   FIRST NAME   MI

2 DATE OF BIRTH

MONTH	DAY	YEAR
Jan		
Feb		
Mar		
Apr		
May		
June		
July		
Aug		
Sept		
Oct		
Nov		
Dec		

3 SOCIAL SECURITY NO.

Right Mark: ●
Wrong Marks: ⊘ ⊗ ◔

4 ETHNIC DESCRIPTION
- American Indian/ Alaskan Native
- Asian/Pacific Islander
- Black/African Amer.
- Canadian Aboriginal
- Caucasian/White
- Chicano/Mex. Amer.
- Hispanic
- Puerto Rican
- Other

5 GENDER
- Male
- Female

6 DOMINANT LANGUAGE
- English
- Other

7 ENGLISH FLUENCY
- Yes
- No

8 CENTER NUMBER

9 TEST FORM CODE

10 TEST BOOK SERIAL NO.

11 TEST FORM

12 TEST DATE

MONTH / DAY / YEAR

13 PLEASE PRINT ALL INFORMATION

LAST NAME   FIRST

MAILING ADDRESS

SOCIAL SECURITY/ SOCIAL INSURANCE NO.

═══ LAW SCHOOL ADMISSION TEST ═══

MARK ONE AND ONLY ONE ANSWER TO EACH QUESTION. BE SURE TO FILL IN COMPLETELY THE SPACE FOR YOUR INTENDED ANSWER CHOICE. IF YOU ERASE, DO SO COMPLETELY. MAKE NO STRAY MARKS.

SECTION 1 / *SECTION 2* / *SECTION 3* / *SECTION 4* / *SECTION 5*

Questions 1–30, each with answer choices (A) (B) (C) (D) (E)

NOTE: If you have a new address, you must write Law Services at Box 2000-C, Newtown, PA 18940 or call (215) 968-1001. We cannot guarantee that all address changes will be processed before scores are mailed, so be sure to notify your post office of your forwarding address.

FOR LAW SERVICES USE ONLY

LR

LW

LCS

SECTION I

Time—35 minutes

25 Questions

Directions: The questions in this section are based on the reasoning contained in brief statements or passages. For some questions, more than one of the choices could conceivably answer the question. However, you are to choose the best answer; that is, the response that most accurately and completely answers the question. You should not make assumptions that are by commonsense standards implausible, superfluous, or incompatible with the passage. After you have chosen the best answer, blacken the corresponding space on your answer sheet.

1. Sea turtle hatchlings leaving their hatching grounds on Florida beaches reach ocean currents by swimming to the northeast, as defined by the north of the Earth's magnetic field. Florida hatchlings placed in a large indoor tank also swim toward the northeast. But when the tank is surrounded by an artificial magnetic field twice as strong as the Earth's field and opposite in direction, the hatchlings swim in the direction opposite to that in which they swim without the artificial magnetic field.

   The information in the statements above most strongly supports which one of the following?

   (A) Once baby sea turtles reach the open sea, they join groups of adults in the North Atlantic.
   (B) The direction in which ocean currents flow is determined by the magnetic field of the Earth.
   (C) Baby sea turtles are able to sense the magnetic field of the Earth.
   (D) No sea turtle ever returns to the beach where it hatched.
   (E) If a sea turtle hatches on the coast of Africa, it will swim toward the southwest.

2. Twenty percent of the population of Springhill has been to Italy at least once in the last five years, and thirty percent of the population of Springhill has been to France at least once in the last five years. Therefore, half of the population of Springhill has been to Europe at least once in the last five years.

   The argument is faulty because it ignores the possibility that

   (A) some of the population of Springhill has been neither to Italy nor to France in the last five years
   (B) some of the population of Springhill has been both to Italy and to France in the last five years
   (C) some of the population of Springhill has been either to Italy or to France in the last five years, but not to both
   (D) none of the population of Springhill has been to any country in Europe other than Italy or France in the last five years
   (E) none of the population of Springhill has been either to Italy or to France more than once in the last five years

Questions 3–4

McBride: The proposed new fuel-efficiency standards, if implemented, will discourage the manufacture of full-size cars. This prospect is troubling because when a subcompact and a full-size car collide, the people in the subcompact are more likely to be seriously injured than if theirs had also been a full-size car. The new fuel-efficiency standards should therefore be opposed.

Leggett: But whenever any two cars collide, it is more likely that someone will be seriously injured if one of the cars is a full-size car than if neither car is full-size. So the new fuel-efficiency standards should be supported precisely because they discourage the manufacture of full-size cars.

3. McBride's and Leggett's statements commit them to disagreeing about the truth of which one of the following?

   (A) The manufacture of full-size cars should be discouraged.
   (B) Fuel conservation is less important than safety in case of a collision.
   (C) When a full-size car and a subcompact car collide, the occupants of the full-size car are less likely than the occupants of the subcompact car to be seriously injured.
   (D) Reducing the number of full-size cars on the highway will reduce the frequency of collisions between automobiles.
   (E) The new fuel-efficiency standards will encourage automobile manufacturers to build more subcompact cars.

4. Which one of the following argumentative strategies does Leggett use in attempting to refute McBride's position?

   (A) demonstrating that McBride's claims are contradictory
   (B) challenging the unstated assumption that all cars are either full-size or subcompact
   (C) shifting the perspective from which the issue of automobile safety is considered
   (D) raising doubts about the accuracy of a generalization made by McBride
   (E) demonstrating that it is impossible to follow the course of action advocated by McBride

GO ON TO THE NEXT PAGE.

5. Concerns for the environment have led chemists to develop plastics that are degradable. All degradable plastics, which are potentially useful packaging materials, need just the right conditions to break down. Some need exposure to sunlight, some need to be buried in soil and some need to be submerged in water. It should be cautioned that some degradable plastics leave residues of unknown toxicity.

If all of the statements above are true, which one of the following must also be true?

(A) Some materials that are potentially useful for packaging leave residues of unknown toxicity.

(B) Some degradable plastics need both sunlight and submersion in order to break down.

(C) Some materials that need sunlight in order to break down are not potentially useful packaging materials.

(D) Some materials that leave residues of unknown toxicity are not degradable plastics.

(E) Some materials that need to be buried in soil to break down leave residues of unknown toxicity.

Questions 6–7

The coming economic recovery will surely be strong. Most of the economists in investment companies now agree that this is so, though the leading academic economists still think otherwise. Since the investment companies' economists are risking their jobs when they make forecasts, whereas academic economists have lifelong tenure, it generally makes sense to take the investment companies' economists more seriously.

6. The main conclusion of the argument is supported only

(A) by comparing the number of experts who agree with the conclusion with the number who disagree with the conclusion

(B) through an assessment of the likely risks and consequences of believing one or another strand of expert opinion

(C) through projection from the economic prospects for investment companies to the economic prospects for the economy as a whole

(D) through an assessment of the relative reliability of the experts who agree with the conclusion as compared with that of those who disagree

(E) by attacking the character of those experts who disagree with the conclusion

7. Which one of the following, if true about the predictions of investment companies' economists, most seriously weakens the argument?

(A) Their content is likely to be dictated as much by the interests of the economist's employer as by an objective assessment of the economy.

(B) They are likely to have more effect on the economic climate than are the predictions of academic economists.

(C) The methods used in arriving at them include factors not employed by academic economists.

(D) Their accuracy is an important factor affecting the profitability of the investment companies.

(E) They are more reliable when they disagree with than when they agree with the predictions of academic economists.

GO ON TO THE NEXT PAGE.

8. John wants to win the annual Mayfield raffle next year because he needs the Mayfield raffle's prize. If he enters more than one raffle next year, the likelihood of his winning one of them would be greater than if he entered only a single raffle. Hence, to have this greater likelihood of winning the Mayfield prize, John should enter several other raffles next year.

The argument exhibits which one of the following flaws in reasoning?

(A) presupposing that a person's strong desire for a certain outcome increases the likelihood that the actual outcome will be as desired

(B) mistaking for the activity itself the goal for which one pursues that activity

(C) assuming without warrant that a person will be successful if the person engages only in those activities that are likely to be successful

(D) assuming that an event, if it is highly improbable, cannot possibly occur

(E) confusing the likelihood that at least one event in a set of events will occur with the likelihood that a designated event in that set will occur

9. In order to avoid causing inadvertent harm to their neighbors, householders ought to evade politely or refuse to answer a stranger's questions regarding their neighbors, unless the stranger provides some proof of being a government official pursuing official inquiries, in which case the questions should be answered truthfully.

In which one of the following situations does Mary act in accordance with the principle above?

(A) A man claiming to be a private detective asked Mary whether her neighbor ever entertained guests overnight. Mary, though unsure of the facts, said that her neighbor never did so, and later told the neighbor about the suspicious questioner.

(B) A stranger showing a police badge asked Mary whether her neighbor was away on vacation. Because several homes in the neighborhood had recently been burglarized while their owners were vacationing, Mary lied and said no.

(C) When asked by a confused-looking couple whether the house next door belonged to a Mr. Brown, who, they said, was expecting them for dinner, Mary answered that it did not, and pointed out Mr. Brown's house.

(D) Immigration officers, showing valid identification and asserting that they were on official business, asked Mary whether a neighbor who belonged to a local church that offered sanctuary to refugees lacking visas had sheltered any such refugees. Mary gave an evasive answer and warned her neighbor.

(E) A woman claiming to be an insurance adjuster asked Mary whether her neighbor owned any vehicles other than the ones currently parked in the neighbor's driveway. Mary answered that the adjuster would have to ask her neighbor as she herself did not really know.

GO ON TO THE NEXT PAGE.

10. Competitive figure skaters are judged by panels of up to nine judges, who use a numerical scale with the highest mark being 6. To arrive at a total score, all judges' marks are summed. Competitive divers are judged by panels of five or seven judges using a scale with 10 as the highest mark. Before all judges' marks are summed to a final score, however, the highest and lowest marks are discarded in order to eliminate the possibility of bias either in favor of or against a particular diver. Competitive figure skating should adopt the approach taken in diving because it is a fairer system.

Which one of the following can be inferred from the passage above?

(A) There is wider disagreement among figure skating judges than among diving judges.
(B) Currently, there is a greater possibility of bias in the scoring process for competitive figure skating than in that for diving.
(C) It is more likely that a diver will receive a biased total score than that a skater will.
(D) It is fairer to judge a competitor on a 10-point scale than a 6-point scale.
(E) Without the discarding of highest and lowest marks, diving would be more vulnerable to bias than figure skating.

11. Rose: The book is either by Deerson or else by Jones; I'm not sure which. However, Deerson's books are generally published by Quince Press, as are Jones's. Therefore, the book is probably published by Quince.

The pattern of reasoning in which one of the following is most similar to that in Rose's argument?

(A) That tree is either a beech or else an elm, and Mercedes can identify most trees, so she will probably be able to tell which it is.
(B) The culprits escaped either by car or else on foot, but in either case they must have opened Isidore's creaking gate. Therefore Isidore probably heard them.
(C) Judging by what he said in the interview, George is either a liar or incredibly naïve. Both these attributes are unsuitable in a customs inspector. Therefore George should not be hired as a customs inspector.
(D) Margarethe the Second was born either in Luppingshavn or else in Kindelberg. Most of the people in each city then were of Mondarian descent, so Margarethe probably had Mondarian ancestors.
(E) Tomás will probably participate in community service, since he will attend either Dunkeld College or Steventon University and at both most students currently enrolled say that they participate in some form of community service.

12. Sarah, who is an excellent mechanic, said that in her opinion the used car John is considering is in good mechanical condition. However, it is clear that Sarah cannot be trusted to give an honest opinion, since when Emmett asked her opinion of his new haircut she lied and said she thought it looked good. Therefore, it is very likely that Sarah also lied in giving her opinion of the mechanical condition of that car.

The argument is flawed by virtue of having committed which one of the following errors of reasoning?

(A) It fails to offer any grounds for the attack it makes on the character of the person.
(B) It confuses claims about the past with claims about the future.
(C) It bases a sweeping claim on the evidence provided by an instance that is not clearly relevant.
(D) It presents evidence in value-laden terms that presuppose the conclusion for which that evidence is offered.
(E) It wrongly assumes that because someone is a competent judge of one kind of thing, that person will be a competent judge of a very different kind of thing.

GO ON TO THE NEXT PAGE.

13. Modern flamingos derive their pink coloration from pigments stored in tiny shrimp that they filter from shallow, salty waters. The shrimp get this pigment from tiny red algae that they filter through their leg bristles. In the Jurassic period (about 200 million years ago), both algae and shrimp were an excellent source of food for any larger animal equipped to sieve them out of the water through an anatomical strainer.

The Argentine pterodactyl possessed a row of thin, bristlelike teeth through which it pumped water, straining out any tiny food particles in the process. Thus, because it was able to filter both algae and shrimp, it is reasonable to conclude that the pterodactyl acquired a pink coloration.

Which one of the following statements, if true, strengthens the argument for the existence of a pink pterodactyl?

(A) The Argentine pterodactyl inhabited the shores of shallow freshwater seas in Jurassic South America.
(B) There is a specific type of shrimp that does not eat the algae immediately but carries them on its bristles and eats them later.
(C) If the Argentine pterodactyl did not eat a diet containing red algae, its color was determined by factors other than diet.
(D) The Argentine pterodactyl's habitat included shallow seas that were particularly rich in red algae and shrimp.
(E) Captive modern flamingos, which do not have access to shallow salty waters from which to filter tiny shrimp, are given a diet that produces a red coloration.

14. In jurisdictions where use of headlights is optional when visibility is good, drivers who use headlights at all times are less likely to be involved in a collision than are drivers who use headlights only when visibility is poor. Yet Highway Safety Department records show that making use of headlights mandatory at all times does nothing to reduce the overall number of collisions.

Which one of the following, if true, most helps to resolve the apparent discrepancy in the information above?

(A) In jurisdictions where use of headlights is optional when visibility is good, one driver in four uses headlights for daytime driving in good weather.
(B) A law making use of headlights mandatory at all times is not especially difficult to enforce.
(C) Only very careful drivers use headlights when their use is not legally required.
(D) There are some jurisdictions in which it is illegal to use headlights when visibility is good.
(E) The jurisdictions where use of headlights is mandatory at all times are those where daytime visibility is frequently poor.

15. Industries waste large amounts of valuable water. Government subsidies allow industries to pay little or nothing for water. Therefore, if industries are required by the government to pay full price for the water they use, inefficient use of water by industry would soon cease altogether.

A flaw in the argument's reasoning is that the argument

(A) presents one possible solution to a problem as the only solution to that problem
(B) bases its conclusion on an ambiguous interpretation of the word "inefficient"
(C) draws a conclusion that is stronger than what is warranted by the evidence presented
(D) assumes what it sets out to prove
(E) offers as evidence considerations that have no relevance to the argument's conclusion

GO ON TO THE NEXT PAGE.

16. When a group of people starts a company, the founders usually serve as sources both of funding and of skills in marketing, management, and technical matters. It is unlikely that a single individual can both provide adequate funding and be skilled in marketing, management, and technical matters. Therefore, companies founded by groups are more likely to succeed than companies founded by individuals.

Which one of the following is an assumption required by the argument?

(A) A new company is more likely to succeed if every founding member contributes equally to the company's initial funding than if some members contribute more funds than others.
(B) Some founding members of successful companies can provide both funding and skills in marketing, management, or technical matters.
(C) New companies are more likely to succeed when their founders can provide adequate funding and skills in marketing, management, and technical abilities than if they must secure funding or skills from nonfounders.
(D) Founders of a new company can more easily acquire marketing and management abilities than technical abilities.
(E) A new company is more likely to succeed if its technical experts are also skilled in management and marketing than if they lack management or marketing skills.

17. Dead, rotting logs on the forest floor provide the habitat for a small mammal, the red-backed vole, which subsists almost entirely on the portion of certain specialized fungi which grows aboveground. The fungi-spores are deposited on the forest floor by the voles. Some of the fungi that develop from these spores form underground sheaths around the fine roots of growing trees, and assist the trees by processing and sharing nutrients and producing an antibiotic which protects the trees from disease.

The information above provides the most support for which one of the following conclusions?

(A) The presence of rotting logs on a forest floor can have beneficial effects on the trees around them.
(B) The red-backed vole is usually able to derive nutrients from the spores of the fungi it eats.
(C) Young, growing trees could not survive without the voles to distribute the spores of certain fungi.
(D) The spores of certain fungi cannot remain viable above the ground but must be deposited near the roots of trees.
(E) Dead and decaying trees are the ideal environment for the growth of certain fungi.

Questions 18–19

Mayor Tyler: In 1982 the courthouse that Roseville still needs would have cost $26 million. Now in 1992 the same building is costing the city close to $30 million to build. If the courthouse had been built in 1982 when I first showed how the building would relieve the overcrowding we were experiencing, Roseville would have saved at least $4 million by now.

Councillor Simón: Your own financial reports inform us that $26 million in 1982 dollars is equivalent to $37 million in 1992 dollars. Adding that difference to the money Roseville has saved by not having to maintain an underutilized courthouse for ten years, we can only view the delay as a financial boon for Roseville.

18. A point at issue between Mayor Tyler and Councillor Simón is whether

(A) Roseville will build a courthouse in 1992
(B) $37 million in 1992 dollars is equivalent to $26 million in 1982 dollars
(C) Mayor Tyler is responsible for the city's major financial reports
(D) Roseville actually needed a new courthouse between 1982 and 1992
(E) Roseville would have expended $4 million to maintain a courthouse from 1982 to 1992

19. Which one of the following, if true, most strongly supports Mayor Tyler's conclusion?

(A) A shortage of courtroom space was not experienced until 1990, but from 1984 to 1992 the city spent a substantial amount of money each year to rent extra office space that the new courthouse would have provided.
(B) Roseville had substantially fewer court cases in 1992 than in 1982, but in 1982 the number of court cases was exceptionally large because of challenges to a controversial law passed in 1981 and repealed in 1982.
(C) There was more opposition to the mayor's proposal in 1982 to build a new courthouse than to the proposal in 1992 for the courthouse to be built.
(D) In 1980 Councillor Simón supported a proposal to build a courthouse that would have cost substantially more than $26 million.
(E) In 1987 a prominent judge resigned from office in protest against crowded prison conditions in the Roseville district.

GO ON TO THE NEXT PAGE.

20. In North America there has been an explosion of public interest in, and enjoyment of, opera over the last three decades. The evidence of this explosion is that of the 70 or so professional opera companies currently active in North America, 45 were founded over the course of the last 30 years.

The reasoning above assumes which one of the following?

(A) All of the 70 professional opera companies are commercially viable operations.
(B) There were fewer than 45 professional opera companies that had been active 30 years ago and that ceased operations during the last 30 years.
(C) There has not been a corresponding increase in the number of professional companies devoted to other performing arts.
(D) The size of the average audience at performances by professional opera companies has increased over the past three decades.
(E) The 45 most recently founded opera companies were all established as a result of enthusiasm on the part of a potential audience.

21. Although many seventeenth-century broadsides, popular ballads printed on a single sheet of paper and widely sold by street peddlers, were moralizing in nature, this is not evidence that most seventeenth-century people were serious about moral values. While over half of surviving broadsides contain moralizing statements, and it is known that many people purchased such compositions, it is not known why they did so, nor is it known how their own beliefs related to what they read.

Which one of the following, if true, most strengthens the argument?

(A) Like other forms of cheap seventeenth-century popular literature, surviving broadsides seem mostly to have been of rather low literary quality and to have been written by hack writers.
(B) In many moralizing ballads, the moral content was confined to a single stanza expressing a pious sentiment tacked onto a sensationalized account of crime and adultery.
(C) Some seventeenth-century ballad sellers also sold sermons printed in pamphlet form.
(D) The clergy occasionally stuck broadsides warning about the danger of strong drink on the doors of seventeenth-century alehouses.
(E) Well-educated people of the seventeenth century held broadsides in contempt and considered broadside peddlers to be disreputable vagrants.

22. In casual conversation, people experience little psychological discomfort in admitting that they have some particular character flaw, but only if they consider trivial the flaw to which they admit. Therefore, if in a casual conversation an individual readily admits that he or she has some particular character flaw, the individual must not consider that flaw to be serious.

Which one of the following is an assumption necessary to the argument?

(A) Most character flaws are considered trivial by those who have them.
(B) People admit to having only those character flaws that most other people consider trivial.
(C) In casual conversation, people admit to having character flaws only when they must.
(D) In casual conversation, people readily admit to having a character flaw only when that admission causes them little psychological discomfort.
(E) In casual conversation, people do not speak of things that would give others an unfavorable impression of their character.

23. This semester Professor Popkin will commute to Montreal by plane, leaving every Tuesday and returning to Toronto every Friday. She instructs her travel agent to schedule for her one round-trip that departs from Toronto on the first Tuesday and returns to Toronto on the last Friday of the semester and additional round-trips that depart from and return to Montreal for each weekly commute in between.

Which one of the following, if true, most helps to explain Professor Popkin's instructions to her travel agent regarding the grouping of her flights into round-trips?

(A) Professor Popkin's round-trip tickets are least expensive if each trip is scheduled so that at least one Saturday night intervenes between the departing flight and the returning flight.
(B) A ticket for a round-trip in which the departing flight and the returning flight are separated by several months will cost Professor Popkin more than a ticket for a round-trip in which they are separated by less than one week.
(C) Professor Popkin will be eligible to travel in the first-class section of the plane at no extra charge after she has completed a specified number of round-trips.
(D) If all Professor Popkin's tickets are paid for at one time, she will be eligible for a frequent-traveler discount.
(E) In order for Professor Popkin to receive the lowest possible airfare, each of her round-trips must be paid for at least seven days in advance of the departing flight.

GO ON TO THE NEXT PAGE.

24. The last outdoor drive-in movie theater in Nova Scotia closed recently. The owners claimed that it could not regularly attract large enough audiences to remain viable. However, for an entire week—the final week of the theater's operation, after the announcement of the impending closure—the place was sold out every night and made a healthy profit. Therefore, the owners' claim was clearly false.

Which one of the following contains an error of reasoning most similar to that made in the argument above?

(A) On the many occasions similar to the present when the library's budget was cut, staff layoffs resulted, so even though the administration denies it, the proposed budget cuts are bound to mean staff layoffs.

(B) The proposed cuts in library funding would require reducing the hours of the periodicals room. But that is a room in which many students like to study, so the proposed cuts are bound to stir up considerable opposition.

(C) All of the students who came to the meeting about proposed cuts in library funding were strongly opposed to the cuts, so all of the students currently enrolled must be strongly opposed.

(D) The overall reduction in the university's budget is 10 percent. The library's budget is being cut by 10 percent. Therefore the library's budget cut is fair.

(E) The administration claims that the library's funding must be cut because of last year's poor library fund drive. However the athletic department's budget is being increased. Therefore, the administration's claim must be false.

25. Environmentalist: It takes less energy to make molten glass from recycled glass than from raw materials. Once the recycled glass or raw materials have been turned into molten glass, making bottles from recycled glass follows the same process as making bottles from raw materials. Obviously, soft drink bottlers who make a large percentage of their bottles from recycled glass have significant energy savings. Therefore, by using recycled glass instead of glass made from raw materials, bottlers can lower their costs and benefit the environment at the same time.

Which one of the following is an assumption on which the argument relies?

(A) The process of making bottles from plastic that has been recycled is not significantly more energy efficient than is the process of making bottles from glass that has been recycled.

(B) The amount of glass that is currently recycled each year is enough to supply the major soft drink bottlers with materials for a large percentage of the glass bottles they make that year.

(C) Most consumers are not able to distinguish bottles made from recycled glass from glass bottles made from raw materials.

(D) Purchasing and transport costs are not so much greater for recycled glass than for raw materials that they outweigh the savings in energy costs resulting from the use of recycled glass.

(E) The process of making molten glass from recycled glass requires fewer steps than does the process of making molten glass from raw materials.

S T O P

IF YOU FINISH BEFORE TIME IS CALLED, YOU MAY CHECK YOUR WORK ON THIS SECTION ONLY.
DO NOT WORK ON ANY OTHER SECTION IN THE TEST.

SECTION II

Time—35 minutes

27 Questions

Directions: Each passage in this section is followed by a group of questions to be answered on the basis of what is <u>stated</u> or <u>implied</u> in the passage. For some of the questions, more than one of the choices could conceivably answer the question. However, you are to choose the <u>best</u> answer; that is, the response that most accurately and completely answers the question, and blacken the corresponding space on your answer sheet.

Historian Philippe Aries claimed that in medieval Europe childhood was not viewed as a distinct period in human development, with a special character and needs. His argument for this (5) thesis relied heavily on medieval text illustrations, which distinguish children from adults principally by their stature, rather than by a distinctively childlike appearance: the children look like miniature adults. Ariès also suggested that high (10) infant mortality rates in the Middle Ages induced indifference toward offspring as a defense mechanism against establishing close ties with infants unlikely to survive. Shulamith Shahar's recent research challenges this established (15) conception of the medieval view of childhood.

Shahar has had to work hard to find evidence to support her interpretation of the medieval conception of childhood, since works that reveal parents' personal attitudes, such as Giovanni (20) Morelli's journal, are exceptional. Shahar makes intelligent use of medical writing and theological works. Particularly illuminating are medieval accounts of saints' lives, which despite their emphasis on personal piety reveal much concerning (25) their subjects' childhoods and which provide evidence of parental concern for children. Even more significant are accounts of saints' miracles involving the healing of sick infants and the blessing of young couples with children.

(30) Shahar also discusses the period in childhood from ages 7 to 11 when boys of the wealthier classes were placed in monasteries or as apprentices in the household of a "master" of a trade. To some this custom might imply a perception of childhood (35) insufficiently distinguished from adulthood, or even indifference to children, evidenced by the willingness to send young children away from home. Shahar points out, however, that training was in stages, and children were not expected to live as (40) adults or to assume all the tasks of maturity at once. Furthermore, Shahar quotes a telling number of instances in which parents of apprentices sued masters for maltreatment of their children. Shahar concludes that parents placed their children in (45) monasteries or as apprentices not to be rid of them, but because it was a social norm to ensure one's children a future niche in society.

Shahar's work is highly persuasive, but as a rebuttal to Ariès, it is uncomfortably incomplete. (50) Shahar succeeds in demonstrating that people in

the Middle Ages did view childhood as a definite stage in human development and that they were not indifferent toward their children. But central to Ariès' position was the contention that the family as (55) a powerful and private institution organized around children is a relatively modern ideal, whose origins Ariès related to the growing influence of the middle classes in the postmedieval period. Ariès felt that this implied something novel about the (60) development of perceptions of childhood and of the family. Shahar does not comment on these larger issues.

1. The passage is primarily concerned with

(A) criticizing and dismissing a traditional theory
(B) describing and evaluating recent research
(C) reconciling two explanations for the same phenomenon
(D) refuting a recent hypothesis
(E) summarizing information about an unusual phenomenon

2. The passage supports which one of the following statements about the treatment of childhood in medieval documents?

(A) Medieval accounts of childhood tend to emphasize the piety of their subjects.
(B) Medieval accounts of saints' lives focus on stories of miracles rather than on the childhood of their subjects.
(C) Medical and theological writings provide scant evidence of parental concern for children.
(D) In medieval text illustrations, children were distinguished from adults by their appearance rather than by their stature.
(E) In medieval text illustrations, children were not depicted with childlike features.

GO ON TO THE NEXT PAGE.

3. Which one of the following best describes the function of the first paragraph of the passage?

    (A) It presents important evidence that a traditional theory has failed to take into account.
    (B) It describes the historical sources that have been the focus of a recent debate.
    (C) It describes an argument that will be challenged by evidence provided in the passage.
    (D) It describes a puzzling historical phenomenon that will be accounted for in the passage.
    (E) It summarizes important information about the historical period that is discussed in the passage.

4. In the third paragraph, the author mentions the period in childhood from ages 7 to 11 most likely in order to

    (A) compare perceptions of childhood in the Middle Ages with perceptions of childhood in the postmedieval period
    (B) suggest that Shahar was unaware of important social norms in medieval communities
    (C) show how Shahar supports her argument about the conception of childhood in the Middle Ages
    (D) suggest that class and gender had important effects on the way in which children were treated in the Middle Ages
    (E) point out the differences between medieval and modern conceptions of children's role in the family

5. Which one of the following, if true, would provide the LEAST support for Shahar's arguments as they are described in the passage?

    (A) Medieval documents contain stories of children, seemingly stillborn, who were miraculously restored to life by the intercession of saints.
    (B) The children of peasants remained at home in the later stages of childhood, gradually taking on more serious tasks until the time came for marriage.
    (C) Impoverished parents left their children at foundling hospitals because they were confident that their children would be better cared for there than they would have been at home.
    (D) The details of the saints' childhoods in the accounts of saints' lives were invented by medieval writers and did not reflect the attitudes of parents in the Middle Ages.
    (E) Parents in the wealthier classes who did not place their children as apprentices were criticized for not providing their children with a secure future.

6. It can be inferred from the passage that Ariès would be likely to agree with all of the following statements EXCEPT:

    (A) Parents in the Middle Ages felt indifferent toward their children.
    (B) Conceptions of childhood and the family changed in the postmedieval period as a result of the growing influence of the middle classes.
    (C) The ideal of the family as a powerful and private institution developed in the Middle Ages.
    (D) People in the Middle Ages viewed their children as miniature adults.
    (E) The family in the Middle Ages was not organized around the children.

7. Shahar's work as it is described in the passage does NOT provide an answer to which one of the following questions?

    (A) Did parents feel affection for their children in spite of the fact that many infants were unlikely to survive?
    (B) How did social norms influence parents' decisions about their children's futures?
    (C) How did the changing perception of the family in the Middle Ages affect the perception of childhood?
    (D) Were parents concerned about their children when they reached the ages of 7 to 11?
    (E) Did parents in the Middle Ages view childhood as a distinct stage in human development?

8. The author would most likely agree with which one of the following statements about Shahar's research in relation to Ariès' theories about childhood in the Middle Ages?

    (A) Shahar's research challenges some of Ariès' arguments, but it does not refute his central position.
    (B) Shahar's research is provocative, but it does not add anything to Ariès' arguments.
    (C) Shahar's research effectively refutes Ariès' central position and presents a new interpretation of childhood and the family in the Middle Ages.
    (D) Shahar's research confirms some of Ariès' arguments but casts doubt on other of Ariès' arguments.
    (E) Shahar's research is highly informative and provides more information about infant mortality rates during the Middle Ages than did Ariès' work.

GO ON TO THE NEXT PAGE.

Increases in the amount of carbon dioxide (CO_2) and other trace gases in the Earth's atmosphere can contribute to what has been called greenhouse warming, because those compounds allow the Sun's
(5) energy to reach the surface of the Earth, thereby warming it, but prevent much of that energy from being reradiated to outer space. Measuring devices set up at several locations around the world have revealed a 20 percent increase in atmospheric CO_2
(10) over the course of the past century—from 290 parts per million in 1880 to 352 parts per million in 1989. Several studies agree that it is plausible that the CO_2 content of the atmosphere may well double from its 1880 level by around the middle of the
(15) twenty-first century.

To project how much the global temperature will increase in response to a doubling of atmospheric CO_2 should be simple: since the CO_2 content has increased by about 20 percent over the past century,
(20) we should be able to observe the increases in global temperature during the same period and base future projections on that data. The prevailing view is that the climatic record over the past century for the entire globe reveals a net increase in
(25) temperature ranging from 0.5 to 1.0 degree Fahrenheit (approximately 0.25 to 0.5 degrees Celsius). But set against this conclusion is the fact that data gathered over the past century in North America, where observations are numerous and
(30) accurate, does not confirm such an increase. And even if the temperature rise is real, another puzzle remains: is the rise in global temperatures a natural fluctuation or a result of the increase in greenhouse gases?
(35) Because of inconclusive data and the complexity of the problem, some scientists predict an increase as small as two degrees Fahrenheit (one degree Celsius) in the average global temperature over the next half century, whereas others predict increases
(40) of up to nine degrees Fahrenheit (five degrees Celsius). It makes a great difference whether the actual increase is at the low or high end of this range. Although human beings are probably resilient enough to adapt to the effects of an
(45) increase of approximately two degrees Fahrenheit (one degree Celsius), an increase of nine degrees Fahrenheit (five degrees Celsius) is believed to be the difference in temperature that separates the end of the last great ice age, 12,000 years ago, from
(50) the present.

In light of such uncertainty, the wisest policy is not to forestall action. Steps that make sense for economic or environmental reasons besides greenhouse warming, such as replacing fossil-fuel
(55) energy with solar energy, could be taken first, whether or not climate warming is taking place. Then, as scientific knowledge grows and uncertainties are reduced, more costly measures could be taken, if warranted, hence closely tying
(60) policy decisions to the latest information available. Scientists and others have aptly called this type of action a "no regrets" policy.

9. Which one of the following statements best expresses the main idea of the passage?

(A) Approaching the problem of greenhouse warming with a "no regrets" policy encourages government agencies to implement affordable but most likely ineffective measures.

(B) Inconclusive data concerning the rise in global temperature over the next half century suggests that politicians should wait until all uncertainties are resolved before taking action.

(C) Costly measures must be taken soon to prevent further increases in greenhouse gases and thus a dangerous rise in global temperatures.

(D) Given the lack of agreement about the effects of greenhouse gases on global temperature, the best policy is to implement sensible measures now and respond to new scientific knowledge as it appears.

(E) Scientists would be able to provide a more accurate estimate of the probable effects of greenhouse warming over the next half century if politicians took steps now to eliminate other environmental problems that contribute to global warming.

10. The passage suggests that a rise in global temperature over the next half century, if it occurs, could result from

(A) a natural climatic variation
(B) an increase in solar reradiation
(C) a 20 percent decrease in atmospheric CO_2 from current levels
(D) a decrease in trace gases in the atmosphere
(E) the replacement of fossil-fuel energy with solar energy

11. Which one of the following best describes the organization of the passage?

(A) A scientific problem is described, discrepancies among proposed solutions to it are evaluated, and a course of action is recommended.

(B) A scientific dispute is discussed and the case for one side is made, taking into account its political repercussions.

(C) A phenomenon is described, different views of its effects are presented, and a policy taking into account these differences is proposed.

(D) A solution to a scientific puzzle is advanced and its implications for action are discussed.

(E) A generally accepted scientific formula is explained in order to introduce a detailed examination of a case that violates the principle.

GO ON TO THE NEXT PAGE.

12. The author refers to the meteorological data gathered in North America over the past century in order to

(A) show how differing views on the extent of the rise in global temperature can be resolved

(B) argue that any warming detected over the past century has most likely been the result of a natural climatic fluctuation

(C) argue against the prevailing view that the amount of atmospheric CO_2 has increased by about 20 percent over the past century

(D) suggest that there should be more numerous and accurate observation points outside of North America

(E) present evidence that casts doubt on the view that global temperature has increased over the past century

13. It can be inferred that the author of the passage would most likely agree with which one of the following statements about a response to global warming?

(A) The most effective measures that could be undertaken to reverse greenhouse warming are not necessarily the most costly.

(B) Costly measures necessary to combat greenhouse warming should be undertaken only when the rise in temperature begins to exceed human beings' capacity to adapt to such an increase.

(C) Given the current state of knowledge about greenhouse warming, less costly measures should be implemented before expensive measures are tried.

(D) Scientists' uncertainty about the effect of greenhouse warming on global temperature might be resolved more quickly if a "no regrets" policy were embraced.

(E) Any measure intended to reduce greenhouse warming should be implemented only if it also addresses other environmental problems.

14. Which one of the following is most analogous to the course of action recommended in the last paragraph?

(A) In response to uncertain predictions regarding the likelihood that an asteroid will collide with Earth, the government has decided to fund an inexpensive but scientifically valuable program to track asteroids and to determine whether more costly measures are warranted.

(B) Although scientists have not pinpointed how a newly discovered disease is spread, the government has implemented a preventive health program to combat the disease by preventing any likely means by which the disease might be communicated.

(C) In light of uncertain estimates about the remaining amount of fossil-fuel energy on the Earth, the government has set up a costly program to convert all industrial machinery to run on less expensive alternative fuels.

(D) Faced with many discrepant predictions about the depletion of the Earth's ozone layer, the government has decided to adapt the preventive measures suggested by the scientific group that predicted the most rapid depletion.

(E) In response to scientific predictions that a disastrous earthquake is highly probable in a certain region, the government has added new requirements to building codes that require relatively inexpensive modifications of existing structures.

GO ON TO THE NEXT PAGE.

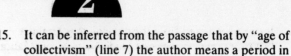
There are two especially influential interpretations of nineteenth-century British feminists' opposition to efforts to restrict women's hours of work: that of liberal legal historians on the
(5) one hand and that of labor historians on the other. For legal historians, the nineteenth century was an "age of collectivism," in which an emphasis on welfare replaced the emphasis on individual rights, and the state came to be seen as a protector of its
(10) inhabitants rather than as a "referee" among citizens. Women and children were the first beneficiaries of maximum-hours restrictions that would eventually spread to men as well. British feminists, according to these scholars, could not
(15) afford to seem to favor these "special" laws for women because their single-minded campaign for women's suffrage relied so heavily on arguments derived from eighteenth-century theories of individual rights and equality. Most labor historians,
(20) on the other hand, explain the feminist opposition to protective laws as coming from middle-class women who blindly ignored the injustices against which such laws' supporters struggled continuously. Labor historians attack the feminists for having a
(25) selfish ideology, one that asked that privileged women be allowed to enjoy equal treatment with privileged men, but not that the economic bases of social relations be rethought.

Recently, however, feminist historians have
(30) begun to uncover plentiful reasons for feminist mistrust of government and trade-union efforts to protect women. Their studies of women's trade unions reveal, as the earlier histories did not, the tensions between women and men within the
(35) trade-union movement. They document that male-dominated trade unions often supported, and sometimes even sponsored, protective labor legislation aimed at forcibly excluding women from wage labor, either in order to maintain a husband's
(40) right to his wife's unpaid labor in the home or to preserve jobs for men. Such gender conflicts were complicated, as other feminist scholars have demonstrated, by self-interested government policies that alternately enticed women into jobs in
(45) order to end labor shortages or pushed them out to provide jobs for men. Finally, the studies show that state labor policy toward women was always deeply influenced by a desire to control female morality and to influence child-bearing decisions.
(50) Whether protective labor legislation for women is just or expedient is still in dispute today, and legal scholars disagree on what criteria to use to evaluate such laws. The labor historians' class-based analyses are no more fully adequate than the liberal legal
(55) historians' benign evolutionary depictions. Feminist historians have a major contribution to make to both the reconstruction of the historical record dealing with women and labor legislation and to broader theories of law as an instrument of social
(60) control and of social change.

15. It can be inferred from the passage that by "age of collectivism" (line 7) the author means a period in which

(A) coalitions among various social classes began to be established in order to promote common legislative goals
(B) legislators began to treat workers as members of a social class rather than as individuals when drafting labor legislation
(C) the competing interests of the various social classes were commonly harmonized by subordinating them to the needs of the state
(D) only needs and goals common to all classes in society became part of society's legislative agenda
(E) the state's role as active promoter of social welfare took precedence over its role as guarantor of individual liberties

16. The passage suggests that histories of nineteenth-century British protective labor laws written by liberal legal historians would be most likely to differ from those written by labor historians in which one of the following ways?

(A) The former would represent such laws as the gradual outgrowth of a general shift in societal ideas; the latter would represent such laws as hard-won reforms that were resisted by powerful elites.
(B) The former would analyze the philosophical underpinnings of arguments in favor of such laws; the latter would dismiss the practical consequences of such laws for those who espoused them.
(C) The former would approve of the motives of feminists who opposed such laws; the latter would refuse to consider seriously the ideology of such feminists.
(D) The former would dispute the existence of inequities in nineteenth-century British society; the latter would examine the historical record carefully in order to highlight such injustices.
(E) The former would portray the effects of such laws as overwhelmingly beneficial; the latter would treat such laws somewhat unsympathetically because of the laws' negative impact on many workers.

GO ON TO THE NEXT PAGE.

17. It can be inferred from the passage that feminist historians believe that one inadequacy of most labor historians' studies of nineteenth-century feminist opposition to protective labor legislation for women was that the studies

    (A) minimized the contribution of enlightened members of the middle class to the passage of such laws
    (B) ignored the philosophical shift in women's perceptions of the state's role that preceded these laws
    (C) overlooked the disadvantages such laws may have presented for nineteenth-century working-class women
    (D) misread the degree to which nineteenth-century feminists focused exclusively on obtaining the vote
    (E) underestimated the potential benefits working-class women would have derived from political equality with men

18. The author implies that liberal legal historians believe that British feminists withheld support from laws restricting women's working hours for which one of the following reasons?

    (A) The feminists felt that society would not benefit from such laws until such laws were drafted to include everyone who worked.
    (B) The feminists feared such support would undermine their arguments in favor of women's suffrage.
    (C) The feminists were unaware of the contributions such laws could make to improving the quality of life of women workers.
    (D) The feminists believed that the enfranchisement of women was the quickest way to prevent the exploitation of women workers.
    (E) The feminists feared that special laws for women, however beneficial, would be a prelude to other laws that restricted women's rights.

19. The author's characterization of the views of labor historians as "class-based" (line 53) most strongly suggests that such historians

    (A) dismissed philosophical arguments deriving from concepts of individual liberty that ignore class
    (B) tended to limit their arguments to those that can be used to promote the interests of the working classes
    (C) were willing to equate gender and class by according women the status of a separate class within society
    (D) relied on historical explanations that depend on the supposed class allegiance of various individuals and groups
    (E) asserted that an unjust political and economic system was responsible for the oppression suffered by the working classes

20. According to the passage, studies by feminist historians suggest that British feminists opposed both nineteenth-century protective labor laws for women and government labor policies primarily for which one of the following reasons?

    (A) Feminist support for such laws and policies could be construed as evidence of philosophical inconsistency, given feminist arguments in favor of women's suffrage.
    (B) Such laws and policies were often intended primarily to promote the interests of male workers or the British government rather than the interests of women workers.
    (C) Women trade unionists actively solicited feminist support in the campaign against such laws and policies because they could find few allies among male trade unionists.
    (D) The potential impact of such laws and policies on women workers had not been recognized by legislators, who, according to feminists, should instead have focused on promoting women's well-being by enfranchising them.
    (E) Male trade unionists, who had previously earned feminist hostility by ignoring the demands of women trade unionists and excluding them from decision-making, favored such laws and policies.

GO ON TO THE NEXT PAGE.

Richard L. Jackson's most recent book, *Black Writers in Latin America*, continues the task of his previous project, *The Black Image in Latin American Literature*. But whereas the earlier work examined
(5) ethnic themes in the writings of both black and non-black authors, the new study examines only black writers living in Latin America (that is, African Hispanic writers). Consequently, there is a shift in emphasis. While the earlier book studied
(10) various attitudes toward black people in Latin America as revealed in a wide range of literature, the later work examines the black representation of black consciousness in Spanish American literature from the early nineteenth century to the present.
(15)   In *Black Writers in Latin America*, Jackson states that "personal identification with blackness and personal experience with the black experience have a great deal to do with a black writer's choice of words, symbols, and images." He goes on to argue
(20) that only black writers have the necessary insight and mastery of the appropriate techniques to depict their situation authentically. In this regard, Jackson joins a number of other North American critics who tend to conceptualize African Hispanic literature as
(25) culturally autonomous, with its own style and themes deriving primarily from the experience of oppression in African Hispanic history. Critics influenced by the Latin American ideal of racial blending, on the other hand, believe that black and
(30) non-black writers share the same cultural context and that, given comparable talent, both are equally equipped to overcome their ethnocentrism. Although Jackson clearly embraces the North American perspective, he does concede in his
(35) introduction that most African Hispanic writers espouse integration rather than separatism.
   At times Jackson's own analysis reveals the problems inherent in using ethnicity as the primary basis for critical judgment: the textual evidence he
(40) cites sometimes subverts the intent to find common tendencies among all writers of a particular racial group. For example, in his chapter on Nicolás Guillén, Jackson attempts to dissociate the black Cuban poet from the Negrista movement, claiming
(45) that "rather than associate Guillén with poetic Negrism, we should see his dramatic conversion to blackness in the late 1920s and early 1930s as a reaction against this white literary fad that was sweeping the world." Admittedly, several of
(50) Guillén's poems from the 1920s show an awareness of social ills like poverty, unemployment, and racial discrimination that is absent from the work of peers influenced by the Negrista movement. But it is difficult to argue that Guillén's portraits of black
(55) people in poems from the early 1930s such as "Canto negro" and "Rumba" are more authentic and less superficial than those in Luis Palés Matos's "Danza negra" or Emilio Ballagas's "Elegía de María Belén Chacón." This effort to distance
(60) Guillén from his Hispanic colleagues thus fails, given the very texts Jackson uses to demonstrate his points.

21. According to the passage, which one of the following is true of Jackson's earlier study of African Hispanic literature?

(A) It discusses the black experience as it is revealed in the works of African Hispanic writers exclusively.
(B) It considers diverse views about black people found in the works of both black and non-black writers.
(C) It examines the representation of black identity in almost two centuries of Spanish American literature.
(D) It focuses on the North American conception of African Hispanic literature.
(E) It emphasizes themes of integration in the works of both black and non-black writers.

22. Which one of the following, if true, would most seriously undermine Jackson's use of ethnicity as a basis for critical judgment of African Hispanic literature?

(A) Several nineteenth-century authors whose novels Jackson presents as reflecting the black experience in Latin America have been discovered to have lived in the United States before moving to Central America.
(B) Luis Palés Matos, Emilio Ballagas, and several other Hispanic poets of the Negrista movement have been shown to have plagiarized the work of African Hispanic poets.
(C) It has been discovered that African Hispanic authors in Latin America over the last two centuries usually developed as writers by reading and imitating the works of other black writers.
(D) A significant number of poems and novels in which early-twentieth-century Hispanic writers consider racial integration have been discovered.
(E) Several poems that are presented by Jackson as authentic portraits of the black experience have been discovered to be misattributed to black poets and can instead be traced to non-black poets.

23. Which one of the following best describes the organization of the second paragraph?

(A) A point of view is described and then placed in context by being compared with an opposing view.
(B) A point of view is stated, and contradictory examples are cited to invalidate it.
(C) A point of view is explained, related to the views of others, and then dismissed as untenable.
(D) A point of view is cited and, through a comparison with another view, is shown to depend on a faulty assumption.
(E) A point of view is put forward, shown to lack historical perspective, and then juxtaposed with another view.

GO ON TO THE NEXT PAGE.

24. According to the passage, which one of the following is true of some of Nicolás Guillén's poems from the 1920s?

(A) They contain depictions of black people that are less realistic than those in the works of non-black poets.
(B) They show greater attention to certain social ills than do poems by his contemporaries.
(C) They demonstrate that Guillén was a leading force in the founding of the Negrista movement.
(D) They are based on Guillén's own experience with racial discrimination, poverty, and unemployment.
(E) They served as stylistic and thematic models for poems by Luis Palés Matos and Emilio Ballagas.

25. It can be inferred that the author of the passage would most likely agree with which one of the following statements concerning an author's capacity to depict the African Hispanic experience?

(A) Validating only the representations of African Hispanic consciousness found in works written by black writers is a flawed approach because many of the most convincing portraits of any racial group are produced by outsiders.
(B) African Hispanic writers, because of their personal experience with African Hispanic culture, are uniquely capable of depicting authentic black characters and experiences.
(C) While seeking an authentic representation of the African Hispanic experience in the works of black writers may provide valuable insights, it is fallacious to attribute authenticity solely on the basis of the race of the author.
(D) Although both black and non-black writers are equally capable of representing the African Hispanic experience, their contributions to African Hispanic literature should be considered separately.
(E) The styles and themes relating to the African Hispanic experience that are found in writings by black authors should serve as the models by which writings by non-black authors are judged for their authenticity.

26. Which one of the following approaches to a study of Hungarian identity in painting is most analogous to the North American approach to African Hispanic literature?

(A) Paintings by ethnic Hungarians and by foreigners living in Hungary should comprise the major focus of the study.
(B) Paintings by ethnic Hungarians and the aspects of those paintings that make their style unique should provide the central basis for the study.
(C) Paintings by Hungarians and non-Hungarians that are most popular with the Hungarian people should comprise the central basis for the study.
(D) The central focus of the study should be to find ways in which ethnic Hungarian painters conform to worldwide artistic movements in their works.
(E) The most important theme in the study should be how paintings created by ethnic Hungarians express universal human concerns.

27. Which one of the following statements best expresses the main idea of the passage?

(A) A central feature of Jackson's approach to African Hispanic literature, shared by some other critics, can be shown to have significant weaknesses.
(B) Jackson's reliance on the Latin American perspective of racial blending and integration in his analysis of African Hispanic literature leads him to make at least one flawed argument.
(C) The African Hispanic authors, poets, and texts that Jackson chooses to analyze in his most recent book are unrepresentative of Spanish American literature and thus lead him to faulty conclusions.
(D) Jackson's emphasis on black writers' contributions to African Hispanic literature in his latest book undercuts the assumptions underlying his own previous work on Spanish American literature.
(E) Jackson's treatment of Guillén reveals a misplaced effort to integrate African Hispanic writers into worldwide literary movements.

S T O P

IF YOU FINISH BEFORE TIME IS CALLED, YOU MAY CHECK YOUR WORK ON THIS SECTION ONLY.
DO NOT WORK ON ANY OTHER SECTION IN THE TEST.

SECTION III

Time—35 minutes

25 Questions

Directions: The questions in this section are based on the reasoning contained in brief statements or passages. For some questions, more than one of the choices could conceivably answer the question. However, you are to choose the best answer; that is, the response that most accurately and completely answers the question. You should not make assumptions that are by commonsense standards implausible, superfluous, or incompatible with the passage. After you have chosen the best answer, blacken the corresponding space on your answer sheet.

1. Historian: Megapolis was once administered wisely, with vision and with universal public support. That's how it became a great city.

    City council member: Not so. Megapolis' past glory was achieved not because of greater vision, but because power was concentrated in the hands of autocrats and hence more easily exercised.

    Which one of the following best captures what is at issue in the dispute between the historian and the city council member?

    (A)   whether Megapolis was once a great city
    (B)   what the best explanation is for Megapolis' past glory
    (C)   whether vision and wisdom are important in urban administration
    (D)   whether the administration of Megapolis once had popular support
    (E)   why Megapolis is no longer a well-run city

2. The striking similarities between Greek temples and subsequent Roman villas testify to the fact that great architects typically draw inspiration from the work of other architects. Such drawing of inspiration does not mean, however, a slavish lack of originality; building according to formulas does not make good buildings. When formulas are used, the results are either bland or disastrous. By contrast, a great architect creates fresh architectural compositions out of familiar forms and synthesizes past and present into a new, richer whole.

    Which one of the following can be inferred from the passage?

    (A)   Roman architects designed many buildings with little or no originality of thought.
    (B)   The essence of good architecture is faithful reproduction of established models.
    (C)   Buildings with unfamiliar forms are likely to be either bland or architectural disasters.
    (D)   Some Roman architecture exemplifies the creation of fresh architectural compositions out of familiar forms.
    (E)   Some Greek temples were not themselves inspired by older models.

3. About two million years ago, lava dammed up a river in western Asia and caused a small lake to form. The lake existed for about half a million years. Bones of an early human ancestor were recently found in the ancient lake-bottom sediments that lie on top of the layer of lava. Therefore, ancestors of modern humans lived in western Asia between two million and one-and-a-half million years ago.

    Which one of the following is an assumption required by the argument?

    (A)   There were no other lakes in the immediate area before the lava dammed up the river.
    (B)   The lake contained fish that the human ancestors could have used for food.
    (C)   The lava that lay under the lake-bottom sediments did not contain any human fossil remains.
    (D)   The lake was deep enough that a person could drown in it.
    (E)   The bones were already in the sediments by the time the lake dried up.

4. A few people who are bad writers simply cannot improve their writing, whether or not they receive instruction. Still, most bad writers can at least be taught to improve their writing enough so that they are no longer bad writers. However, no one can become a great writer simply by being taught how to be a better writer, since great writers must have not just skill, but also talent.

    Which one of the following can be properly inferred from the passage above?

    (A)   All bad writers can become better writers.
    (B)   All great writers had to be taught to become better writers.
    (C)   Some bad writers can never become great writers.
    (D)   Some bad writers can become great writers.
    (E)   Some great writers can be taught to be even better writers.

GO ON TO THE NEXT PAGE.

Questions 5–6

Paretan newspaper editor: David Salino assails as distorted our quotation of remarks on Paretan values by the Qinkoan prime minister and bemoans what he sees as the likely consequences for Paretan-Qinkoan relations. Those consequences will not be our fault, however, since officials at the Qinkoan embassy and scholars at the Institute of Qinkoan Studies have all confirmed that, as printed, our quotation was an acceptable translation of the prime minister's remarks. No newspaper can fairly be blamed for the consequences of its reporting when that reporting is accurate.

5. Which one of the following most accurately expresses the conclusion in the editor's response to David Salino?

(A) What the prime minister said about Paretan values is not a distortion.
(B) Assessing the likely consequences of reporting the prime minister's remarks is irrelevant to the question of whether they ought to have been reported.
(C) The newspaper's rendering of the prime minister's remarks was not inaccurate reporting according to the authorities who are in the best position to judge.
(D) The newspaper cannot be held responsible for the adverse consequences that David Salino claims will likely result from the quotation of the prime minister's remarks in the newspaper.
(E) David Salino's assessment of the likely consequences of reporting the prime minister's remarks is inaccurate.

6. Which one of the following is an assumption on which the editor's argument depends?

(A) The confirmation that the translation is acceptable is sufficient to show that the prime minister's remarks were accurately reported.
(B) Newspapers ought not to consider the consequences of their coverage in deciding what to report.
(C) If the newspaper's rendering of the prime minister's remarks was not distorted, then there is no reason to fear adverse consequences from reporting the remarks.
(D) If David Salino was prepared to praise the newspaper for any favorable consequences of quoting the prime minister's remarks, he could then hold the newspaper to blame for adverse consequences.
(E) Only scholars or people with official standing are in a position to pass judgment on whether a translation of Qinkoan into Paretan is acceptable.

Questions 7–8

Automobile manufacturers who began two decades ago to design passenger vehicles that were more fuel-efficient faced a dilemma in the fact that the lighter, more efficient vehicles were less safe on high-speed highways. However, the manufacturers avoided this dilemma by producing two types of passenger vehicles: a lighter vehicle for medium-speed, local transportation, and a heavier, safer vehicle for long-distance travel. Since most automobile traffic is local, a net savings in fuel use was achieved with no loss in safety.

7. Which one of the following, if true, most strengthens the argument?

(A) Most households whose members do any long-distance driving own at least two passenger vehicles.
(B) There are more cars using high-speed highways today than there were two decades ago.
(C) Even large automobiles are lighter today than similar-sized vehicles were two decades ago.
(D) Most high-speed highways are used by both commercial vehicles and passenger vehicles.
(E) Some automobile manufacturers designed prototypes for fuel-efficient passenger vehicles more than two decades ago.

8. Which one of the following, if true, most seriously weakens the argument?

(A) Lighter vehicles can have smaller, more fuel-efficient engines without sacrificing power.
(B) Long-distance drives are usually made on high-speed highways.
(C) Every automobile manufacturer now produces a greater number of fuel-efficient passenger vehicles than that manufacturer did two decades ago.
(D) Many drivers use high-speed highways even when traveling locally.
(E) Passenger vehicles today weigh less, on average, than did passenger vehicles two decades ago.

GO ON TO THE NEXT PAGE.

9. A scholar discovered an unlabeled nineteenth-century recording of someone reciting a poem written by Walt Whitman. During the nineteenth century, recordings of poetry were not made for wide commercial sale. Rather, they were made either as rare private souvenirs of the voices of famous poets or else as publicity stunts, in which actors recorded poems that were familiar to the public. Since the Whitman poem in the recording was never even published, it is likely that the voice in the recording is actually Whitman's.

The argument proceeds by

(A) offering several pieces of evidence each of which independently points to the same conclusion

(B) distinguishing a phenomenon into two subtypes and then for a particular case eliminating one of those subtypes

(C) offering a general principle and then demonstrating that the general principle is violated in a particular case

(D) showing that two apparently mutually exclusive alternatives are actually compatible with one another

(E) explaining the historical context of an incident in order to demonstrate that each of the two possible scenarios involving that incident is as likely as the other

10. All coffee drinkers in an office ought to contribute equally to the fund that pays for the office's coffee, because, although some coffee drinkers would prefer to pay for their coffee by the cup, or in some other manner, it is better if everyone who drinks the office's coffee provides the same amount of support to the fund.

The reasoning in the argument is most vulnerable to criticism on which one of the following grounds?

(A) It offers, in place of support for its conclusion, a mere restatement of that conclusion.

(B) It overlooks the possibility that what is true under certain specified conditions is not necessarily true under most conditions.

(C) It uses emotionally charged terms to characterize unfairly the position it attempts to refute.

(D) It applies a double standard whereby one group of people is judged wrong and another group judged right for engaging in similar behavior.

(E) It offers two alternatives that do not exhaust the possibilities available and then treats those alternatives as the only possible ones.

11. In 1987 Fabrico, a clothing manufacturer, sold to its customers a total of 2.3 million dollars worth of clothing, a 17 percent increase over 1986 sales. In January 1988, however, Fabrico closed one of its clothing factories, citing reduced demand for its products as the major reason.

Which one of the following, if true about 1987, contributes most to a resolution of the apparent discrepancy noted between the sales figures and the reason offered for closing a factory?

(A) The total worldwide dollar value of clothing sales by manufacturers to customers increased by 5 percent over sales in 1986.

(B) Fabrico's employees dropped earlier demands for a 25 percent increase in company-paid benefits and a 15 percent increase in hourly wages.

(C) Because of escalating costs for raw materials, prices charged by Fabrico for its products were on average 42 percent higher than they were in 1986.

(D) Fabrico introduced several new styles of clothing that were generally praised by fashion critics and that sold very well.

(E) Fabrico spent less on capital improvements than it did in 1986, when it added new plant capacity and new equipment.

12. Gerrit: While browsing in a record store I noticed that one copy of a recording I wanted had mistakenly been priced at a quarter of the list price. When I finally reached the cashier I was told that the price had been mismarked and I would have to pay the full list price. Since I had wasted an hour standing in line, the retailer was morally obligated to sell me the recording at the lower price.

Saskia: I disagree. You knew that a mistake had been made, and you were simply trying to take advantage of that mistake.

Which one of the following principles, if established, would most help to justify Saskia's position?

(A) The price displayed on an item in a retail store morally constitutes an irrevocable offer to sell the item at that price.

(B) Customers of retail stores are morally entitled to profit from any mistakes that the retailers make in marking prices.

(C) Retailers are morally entitled to update marked prices periodically in order to reflect changes in manufacturers' suggested prices.

(D) Retailers are morally obligated to meet expectations about prices that they have intentionally encouraged their customers to hold.

(E) Retailers are morally obligated to sell an item to a customer at a mismarked price only if that customer was genuinely misled about the intended price by the mismarking.

GO ON TO THE NEXT PAGE.

13. Treasure hunter: In general, archaeological artifacts found on public property cannot legally be privately owned. But according to centuries-old maritime law, people who risk their lives attempting to rescue a ship in peril are permitted to keep whatever cargo they can salvage. Under this rule treasure hunters clearly are entitled to keep the cargo from ancient shipwrecks that they risk their lives to save from oblivion in public waters.

Archaeologist: Not so. These shipwrecks have stabilized over the centuries they have lain underwater. The only danger they are in is from greedy treasure hunters who destroy archaeological evidence in their hurry to loot salable artifacts.

On the evidence of their statements, it can be concluded that the treasure hunter and the archaeologist disagree on which one of the following?

(A) what constitutes an archaeological artifact
(B) in what sense, if any, an ancient shipwreck can be said to be in peril
(C) whether treasure hunters risk their lives when they retrieve artifacts from ancient shipwrecks
(D) whether maritime law can ever be applied to a ship that has already sunk
(E) whether antique shipwrecks in public waters can properly be said to be on public property

14. Houseflies kept in small containers at normal room temperature lived for about 50 days. Houseflies kept in identical containers but at a significantly cooler temperature lived longer than 6 months. Apart from longevity, the only difference detected between the groups was that the flies in the colder environment consumed oxygen much more slowly than did those kept at room temperature.

Which one of the following, if true, most helps to explain the difference in the houseflies' life spans?

(A) For flies kept at room temperature, the larger the container the higher the rate of oxygen consumption.
(B) As a fly consumes oxygen, its cells produce a toxic substance that accumulates in the cells until it kills the fly.
(C) There were more containers of flies kept in the colder environment than in the warmer one.
(D) The spiders that prey on flies consume oxygen more slowly in cold weather than in warm weather.
(E) Flies kept in small containers cannot fly, although flying greatly increases a fly's rate of oxygen consumption.

15. It is proposed to introduce mosquitoes into the wild with genetic alterations that destroy their disease-carrying capacity. In this way the dangerous wild population could eventually be replaced by a harmless one without leaving room for another disease-transmitting strain to flourish. One candidate gene would interfere with the mosquitoes' finding mates; another would cause the destruction of a disease parasite before the stage at which it could be transmitted; another would disable the mechanism of the mosquito's own resistance to disease, so that it would die before transmitting the disease.

Which one of the following identifies a discrepancy in the proposal above?

(A) It is presupposed that all three genes would prove equally easy to isolate and insert into the cells of the mosquitoes.
(B) Two of the proposed ways of destroying disease-carrying capacity in the wild mosquito population would jeopardize the goal of the proposal.
(C) It does not take into account positive roles that mosquitoes play in the environment, such as serving, in the larval stage, as food for fish.
(D) None of the three proposed alternatives would assure that there would be fewer mosquitoes in any given area.
(E) Evidence is not presented to show that each alternative method has been successfully tested on a limited scale.

GO ON TO THE NEXT PAGE.

16. Zebra mussels, a nuisance when they clog the intake pipes of nuclear power plants and water plants along the Great Lakes, have some redeeming qualities. Since the mussels feed voraciously on algae that they filter from the water that passes by them, bags of zebra mussels suspended in the discharge streams of chemical plants significantly improve water quality, even removing some hazardous wastes.

Which one of the following is most strongly supported on the basis of the statements above, if they are true?

(A) Zebra mussels arrived in the Great Lakes on transatlantic freighters and, since they have no natural enemies there, are rapidly displacing the native species of clams.

(B) If the mussels spread to areas of the Mississippi River where native clams provide the basis for a cultured-pearl industry, that industry will collapse, since the mussels are unsuitable for such use and would displace the clams.

(C) There is no mechanical means available for clearing intake pipes by scraping the mussels from them.

(D) The algae on which the mussels feed would, if not consumed by the mussels, themselves clog the intake pipes of nuclear power plants and water plants.

(E) Any hazardous waste the mussels remove from chemical-plant discharge will remain in the mussels, if they do not transform it, and they then must be regarded as hazardous waste.

17. Professor Edwards must have revealed information that was embarrassing to the university. After all, to have been publicly censured by the head of the university, as Edwards was, a professor must either have revealed information that embarrassed the university or have been guilty of gross professional negligence, and Edwards' professional behavior is impeccable.

Which one of the following arguments exhibits a pattern of reasoning most similar to that in the argument above?

(A) According to company policy, employees who are either frequently absent without notice or who are habitually late receive an official warning. Since Ms. Jensen has never received such a warning, rumors that she is habitually late must be false.

(B) Any employee of Wilkins, Waddel, and Sloan who discusses a client with a member of the press will be either fired or demoted. But since Wilkins employees never discuss their clients at all, no Wilkins employee will ever be demoted.

(C) Anyone promoted to supervisor must either have worked on the shop floor for three years or have an influential sponsor. Daniels, therefore, clearly has an influential sponsor, since he was promoted to supervisor after only one year on the shop floor.

(D) To earn a merit salary increase, an employee of TGX must either bring in new clients or develop innovative products. No innovative products were developed at TGX this year, however, so TGX employees must have brought in many new clients.

(E) Anyone who is either awarded a letter of commendation or who receives a bonus must be recommended by a company officer. Simon has been recommended by a company officer and will receive a bonus, so he must not have been awarded a letter of commendation.

GO ON TO THE NEXT PAGE.

18. Citizen: Each year since 1970, a new record has been set for the number of murders committed in this city. This fact points to the decreasing ability of our law enforcement system to prevent violent crime.

City official: You overlook the fact that the city's population has risen steadily since 1970. In fact, the number of murder victims per 100 people has actually fallen slightly in the city since 1970.

Which one of the following, if true, would most strongly counter the city official's response?

(A) The incidence of fraud has greatly increased in the city since 1970.
(B) The rate of murders in the city since 1970 decreased according to the age group of the victim, decreasing more for younger victims.
(C) Murders and other violent crimes are more likely to be reported now than they were in 1970.
(D) The number of law enforcement officials in the city has increased at a rate judged by city law enforcement experts to be sufficient to serve the city's increased population.
(E) If the health care received by assault victims last year had been of the same quality as it was in 1970, the murder rate in the city last year would have turned out to be several times what it actually was.

19. Some works of art that today are recognized masterpieces were considered obscene when first created. It therefore follows that what is considered obscene or not obscene has changed over time.

Which one of the following is an assumption on which the argument depends?

(A) Displays of works of art that are considered obscene change the way in which obscenity is defined.
(B) The number of things that are considered obscene has decreased with the passage of time.
(C) Public opinion does not determine the artistic value of a work of art.
(D) Not all currently recognized masterpieces that were once considered obscene are still considered obscene.
(E) All currently recognized masterpieces have at one time been considered obscene.

20. Criminals released from prison on parole have generally been put under routine supervision. A recent program has allowed criminals to leave prison early under intensive supervision; they must obey curfews and in some cases they must be electronically monitored. The percentage of released criminals arrested while under supervision is the same for intensive supervision as for routine supervision, so intensive supervision is no more effective than routine supervision in preventing criminals from committing additional crimes.

Which one of the following is an assumption on which the argument relies?

(A) The criminals under intensive supervision, but not those under routine supervision, were required to work or attend school during their supervision period.
(B) All of the criminals who were arrested while under routine supervision had been in prison more than once before being paroled and put under supervision.
(C) The proportion of arrests to crimes committed was not significantly higher for criminals under intensive supervision than for those under routine supervision.
(D) Of the criminals arrested while under intensive supervision, some would not have committed crimes if they had been under routine supervision.
(E) The number of criminals put under routine supervision was not significantly greater than the number of criminals put under intensive supervision.

GO ON TO THE NEXT PAGE.

Questions 21–22

Bicycle safety expert: Bicycling on the left half of the
    road is much more likely to lead to collisions with
    automobiles than is bicycling on the right. After all,
    in three different studies of bicycle-automobile
    collisions, the bicyclist was riding on the left in 15, 17,
    and 25 percent of the cases, respectively.

Skeptic: But in places where a comparatively high
    percentage of bicyclists used to ride on the left, there
    was surprisingly little decrease in collisions between
    bicyclists and automobiles after bicycling on the left
    was made illegal.

21. One reason the strength of the bicycle safety expert's
     argument cannot be evaluated is that

     (A)   the statistics cited in support of the conclusion
           that bicycling on the left is more likely to lead
           to collisions with automobiles already
           presuppose the truth of that conclusion
     (B)   the statistics it cites do not include the
           percentage of bicycling that took place on the
           left
     (C)   no statistics are provided on the proportion of
           bicycle accidents that are due to bicycle-
           automobile collisions
     (D)   bicycling on the left is singled out for criticism
           without consideration of other bicycling
           practices that are unsafe
     (E)   it does not distinguish between places in which
           bicycling on the left is legal and places in
           which it is illegal

22. Which one of the following statements about places
     that have outlawed bicycling on the left half of the
     road, if true, most helps to resolve the apparent
     discrepancy between the bicycle safety expert's claim
     and the facts cited by the skeptic?

     (A)   These places also have laws about other
           aspects of bicycling safety.
     (B)   These places provide bicycle-safety education
           programs for teenagers.
     (C)   Police officers in these places do not enforce
           regulations that apply to bicyclists.
     (D)   Large numbers of adults as well as children
           ride bicycles in these places.
     (E)   Collisions between bicyclists and automobiles
           constitute about one-quarter of the bicycle
           accidents in these places.

23. Sometimes individuals must choose between two
     courses of action: one that most benefits the
     community and another that most benefits the person
     making the decision. Faced with such a choice,
     individuals tend to choose the course of action most
     beneficial to themselves. It is therefore a principle of
     good government to adjust the incentives and
     disincentives for private individuals so that such
     choices rarely arise, ensuring as far as possible that
     what is the best choice for individuals is the best
     choice for the community.

     Which one of the following best illustrates an
     application of the cited principle of good
     government?

     (A)   In order to escape charges of favoritism, the
           city government awards the contract for a
           new courthouse to a different developer from
           the one who completed the new city hall,
           even though the contract bids from both
           developers were the same.
     (B)   In order to satisfy a powerful law-and-order
           group, the legislature rejects a new bill
           protecting suspects' rights, despite the bill's
           popularity among voters in general.
     (C)   In order to placate laid-off government
           workers who have demanded help in
           acquiring skills necessary for private industry
           jobs, the government diverts funds from
           existing social programs to a new job-training
           program.
     (D)   In order to deflect voter attention from a
           recent increase in the salaries of elected
           officials, the legislature votes against a
           proposal to increase the salaries of appointed
           officials.
     (E)   In order to avoid electricity shortages that will
           occur unless electricity use in the city
           significantly decreases, the city government
           approves an increase in the electricity rate
           charged to city residents.

GO ON TO THE NEXT PAGE.

24. Many professional economists describe economics as a science. Sciences, however, are by definition non-normative: they describe but they do not prescribe. Yet economists are often called on to recommend a course of action for governments and financial institutions. Therefore, since economists play a prescriptive role in society, economics should not be thought of as a science.

The reasoning in the argument is flawed because the argument

(A) treats closely related aspects of a discipline as separate and distinct from each other
(B) attacks the proponents of a claim rather than addressing the merits of the claim itself
(C) insists on a change in terminology when that change would have no practical consequences
(D) fails to recognize the significance of the distinction between a discipline and the people who work within that discipline
(E) overlooks the necessity of divisions of labor within society

25. The Venetian Renaissance painter Vittore Carpaccio used sumptuous reds in most of his paintings. Since the recently discovered Venetian Renaissance painting *Erato Declaiming* contains notable sumptuous reds, it is probably by Carpaccio.

Which one of the following contains a pattern of flawed reasoning most similar to that in the argument above?

(A) Most Renaissance painters worked in a single medium, either tempera or oil. Since the Renaissance painting *Calypso's Bower* is in oil, its painter probably always used oil.
(B) In Italian Renaissance painting, the single most common subject was the Virgin and Child, so the single most common subject in Western art probably is also the Virgin and Child.
(C) Works of art in the Renaissance were mostly commissioned by patrons, so the Renaissance work *The Dances of Terpsichore* was probably commissioned by a patron.
(D) The anonymous painting *St. Sebastian* is probably an early Florentine painting since it is in tempera, and most early Florentine paintings were in tempera.
(E) Since late-Renaissance paintings were mostly in oil, the Venetian late-Renaissance painter Arnoldi, whose works are now lost, probably painted in oil.

S T O P

IF YOU FINISH BEFORE TIME IS CALLED, YOU MAY CHECK YOUR WORK ON THIS SECTION ONLY.
DO NOT WORK ON ANY OTHER SECTION IN THE TEST.

SECTION IV

Time—35 minutes

24 Questions

Directions: Each group of questions in this section is based on a set of conditions. In answering some of the questions, it may be useful to draw a rough diagram. Choose the response that most accurately and completely answers each question and blacken the corresponding space on your answer sheet.

Questions 1–6

An upholsterer will do seven jobs—N, O, P, S, T, U, and X—during a given week on Monday through Friday. Each job is done on exactly one of the days, and no two jobs are done concurrently. Each job takes either one half day or an entire day. The following conditions apply:

N is done on the same day as S.

X is done on Wednesday, and T is done on Friday.

S is done earlier than the day on which P is done.

U and X are the only jobs that must take an entire day each.

1. Which one of the following is an acceptable schedule for the seven jobs?

	Mon.	Tues.	Wed.	Thurs.	Fri.
(A)	N, S	P	X	O, U	T
(B)	O	N, S	X	P	U
(C)	P	U	X	N, S	O, T
(D)	S	N, P	X	U	O, T
(E)	U	N, S	X	O	P, T

2. Which one of the following is a complete and accurate list of those jobs each of which CANNOT be done on Tuesday?

(A) P, U
(B) T, X
(C) N, P, S
(D) N, S, X
(E) T, U, X

3. If O is done on Thursday, N could be done on

(A) Monday, but on no other day
(B) Thursday, but on no other day
(C) Monday or else on Tuesday, but on no other day
(D) Tuesday or else on Wednesday, but on no other day
(E) Wednesday or else on Thursday, but on no other day

4. Which one of the following must be true if the upholsterer does two jobs on Thursday and two jobs on Friday?

(A) N is done on Monday.
(B) O is done on Tuesday.
(C) P is done on Friday.
(D) O is done on the same day as P.
(E) O is done on the same day as T.

5. If P is not done on Friday, which one of the following must be true?

(A) N is done on Monday or else on Thursday.
(B) O is done on Wednesday or else on Thursday.
(C) S is done on Monday or else on Thursday.
(D) P is done on the same day as O.
(E) O is done on the same day as either P or T.

6. If O is done on Monday, which one of the following must be true?

(A) N is done on Tuesday.
(B) P is done on Thursday.
(C) P is done on Friday.
(D) S is done on Thursday.
(E) U is done on Friday.

GO ON TO THE NEXT PAGE.

Questions 7–13

Seven persons—G, H, I, K, L, M, and P—are going rock-climbing together. One person will be the organizer and not a member of any team. The remaining six will form three climbing teams, each consisting of two persons. No person can be on more than one team. The following conditions also apply:

M and P cannot be on the same team as each other.
If K is on a team, M must also be on that team.
If G is on a team, either H or I must also be on that team.
If H is on a team, K must be the organizer.

7. Which one of the following can be a list of the members of the three teams?

 (A) Team 1: G, H; Team 2: I, L; Team 3: M, P
 (B) Team 1: G, H; Team 2: L, P; Team 3: K, M
 (C) Team 1: G, I; Team 2: H, M; Team 3: L, P
 (D) Team 1: G, P; Team 2: I, L; Team 3: K, M
 (E) Team 1: H, M; Team 2: I, L; Team 3: K, P

8. Each of the following is a pair of persons who can constitute a team EXCEPT:

 (A) H, I
 (B) H, M
 (C) I, M
 (D) I, P
 (E) L, P

9. Which one of the following can be the organizer, who is not on any team?

 (A) G
 (B) H
 (C) I
 (D) L
 (E) P

10. If G and I form a team and if H is a member of a team, then H must be on the same team as either

 (A) K or L
 (B) K or P
 (C) L or M
 (D) L or P
 (E) M or P

11. If L and M are on different teams, which one of the following must be true?

 (A) H is the organizer.
 (B) K is the organizer.
 (C) G is on the same team as H.
 (D) I is on the same team as M.
 (E) L is on the same team as P.

12. Which one of the following lists three persons each of whom must be on a team and no two of whom can be on the same team as each other?

 (A) G, L, M
 (B) G, M, P
 (C) H, I, L
 (D) I, L, P
 (E) L, M, P

13. There are how many different persons any one of whom could be paired with M to form a team?

 (A) one
 (B) two
 (C) three
 (D) four
 (E) five

GO ON TO THE NEXT PAGE.

Questions 14–18

A train makes five trips around a loop through five stations—P, Q, R, S, and T, in that order—stopping at exactly three of the stations on each trip. The train must conform to the following conditions:

The train stops at any given station on exactly three trips, but not on three consecutive trips.

The train stops at any given station at least once in any two consecutive trips.

14. Which one of the following could be the list of stations at which the train stops on the first two trips?

   (A) first trip: P, Q, S;   second trip: P, Q, R
   (B) first trip: P, Q, T;   second trip: Q, R, T
   (C) first trip: Q, R, S;   second trip: P, Q, S
   (D) first trip: Q, S, T;   second trip: P, R, S
   (E) first trip: R, S, T;   second trip: P, R, T

15. If on the first and third trips the train is to stop at Q, R, and S, and at R, S, and T, respectively, which one of the following is the list of stations at which it must stop on the second trip?

   (A) P, Q, R
   (B) P, Q, T
   (C) P, S, T
   (D) Q, R, T
   (E) Q, S, T

16. The train CANNOT stop at both P and Q on both the

   (A) first and third trips
   (B) first and fourth trips
   (C) second and fourth trips
   (D) second and fifth trips
   (E) fourth and fifth trips

17. If the train is to stop at Q, R, and T on the first trip and at Q, R, and S on the fourth trip, then it could be true that the train

   (A) stops at Q on the second trip
   (B) stops at R on the fifth trip
   (C) stops at T on the second trip
   (D) does not stop at P on the third trip
   (E) does not stop at T on the fifth trip

18. Suppose that the train's scheduler mistakenly scheduled the train to make the following stops on the first three trips: Q, R, and S on the first trip; P, Q, and S on the second trip; and R, S, and T on the third trip. Which one of the following is a substitution that results in a schedule for those three trips under which the train violates no condition?

   (A) on the first trip, P for Q
   (B) on the second trip, R for S
   (C) on the second trip, T for S
   (D) on the third trip, P for R
   (E) on the third trip, P for S

GO ON TO THE NEXT PAGE.

Questions 19–24

On a certain morning, each of six speakers—Feinberg, Guzman, Harrison, Jansen, Kim, and Mackey—will lecture for exactly one hour. Each lecture will take place in either the library or the studio, with exactly one speaker at a time lecturing in each of these two rooms. The lectures must be given in a manner consistent with the following conditions:

Exactly three of the lectures are given in each room, the first beginning at precisely 8 A.M., the second at precisely 9 A.M., and the third at precisely 10 A.M.
Feinberg's lecture cannot begin earlier than Guzman's.
Neither Jansen's lecture nor Mackey's lecture begins at the same time as Feinberg's.
Harrison's lecture begins earlier than Feinberg's.
Jansen and Mackey, not necessarily in that order, lecture in the studio.

19. Which one of the following must be true?

(A) Either Jansen or else Mackey lectures in the studio beginning at 8 A.M.
(B) Either Harrison or else Mackey lectures in the studio beginning at 9 A.M.
(C) Either Guzman or else Harrison lectures in the library beginning at 8 A.M.
(D) Either Feinberg or else Guzman lectures in the library beginning at 9 A.M.
(E) Either Feinberg or else Guzman lectures in the library beginning at 10 A.M.

20. If both Kim's lecture and Mackey's lecture begin at 9 A.M., which one of the following could be true?

(A) Guzman's lecture begins at 8 A.M.
(B) Harrison's lecture begins at 10 A.M.
(C) Jansen's lecture begins at 10 A.M.
(D) Guzman lectures in the library.
(E) Harrison lectures in the studio.

21. If Harrison's lecture begins at 9 A.M., which one of the following must be true?

(A) Feinberg lectures in the library.
(B) Guzman lectures in the studio.
(C) Harrison lectures in the library.
(D) Kim lectures in the studio.
(E) Mackey lectures in the library.

22. Each of the following is a pair of speakers whose lectures could begin at the same time as each other EXCEPT:

(A) Feinberg and Guzman
(B) Feinberg and Kim
(C) Guzman and Jansen
(D) Guzman and Kim
(E) Guzman and Mackey

23. If Feinberg lectures in the library beginning at 9 A.M., which one of the following could be true?

(A) Guzman lectures in the studio beginning at 10 A.M.
(B) Harrison lectures in the studio beginning at 8 A.M.
(C) Jansen lectures in the studio beginning at 10 A.M.
(D) Kim lectures in the studio beginning at 9 A.M.
(E) Mackey lectures in the studio beginning at 9 A.M.

24. Which one of the following could be a list of the speakers who give their lectures in the studio, in the order in which they give their lectures, from first to third, respectively?

(A) Feinberg, Jansen, Mackey
(B) Guzman, Kim, Mackey
(C) Harrison, Jansen, Kim
(D) Jansen, Mackey, Harrison
(E) Mackey, Feinberg, Jansen

S T O P

IF YOU FINISH BEFORE TIME IS CALLED, YOU MAY CHECK YOUR WORK ON THIS SECTION ONLY.
DO NOT WORK ON ANY OTHER SECTION IN THE TEST.

SIGNATURE _____

LSAT WRITING SAMPLE TOPIC

Tyrone Hodge, a struggling young actor, has just been offered a continuing role in a television soap opera and a supporting role in a new play being staged by a major regional theater. Time constraints prohibit him from accepting both roles. Write an argument in support of one role over the other based on the following criteria:

- Tyrone needs a role that will launch his acting career.
- Tyrone needs enough income to cover both his living expenses and the monthly payment on his substantial college loans.

In the soap opera, which is watched daily by millions of people, Tyrone has been cast in a minor role as a young, unmarried doctor who has just moved into town. The director has told Tyrone that the part could be expanded if viewers respond favorably to his character. Tyrone's weekly salary will be reasonable given his lack of experience and will increase if his role becomes more significant. The director, while known to be difficult, prides herself on nurturing young talent; several of her proteges have gone on to highly successful film and television careers. Last year, the soap opera's ratings fell appreciably, and the show could be canceled if ratings do not improve this season.

A well-known playwright has written a much heralded new play that will have a two-month run at a nationally respected regional theater. The production is certain to be reviewed in the national media. Tyrone has been cast in a supporting role as the leading lady's brother; he has two monologues and spends much of the play onstage. One of the playwright's previous plays went from a regional theater to lengthy runs in New York, Toronto, and London. Another won several prestigious awards but was not a commercial success. His last play closed after one week. Tyrone's salary for the regional theater will be modest and will end, of course, when the play's run is over.

Directions:

1. Use the Answer Key on the next page to check your answers.

2. Use the Scoring Worksheet below to compute your raw score.

3. Use the Score Conversion Chart to convert your raw score into the 120-180 scale.

Scoring Worksheet

1. Enter the number of questions you answered correctly in each section.

	Number Correct
SECTION I	_____
SECTION II	_____
SECTION III	_____
SECTION IV	_____

2. Enter the sum here: _____
   This is your Raw Score.

Conversion Chart
For Converting Raw Score to the 120-180 LSAT Scaled Score
LSAT Form 6LSS29

Reported Score	Raw Score Lowest	Raw Score Highest
180	98	101
179	97	97
178	96	96
177	95	95
176	94	94
175	93	93
174	92	92
173	90	91
172	89	89
171	88	88
170	86	87
169	85	85
168	83	84
167	82	82
166	80	81
165	79	79
164	77	78
163	75	76
162	74	74
161	72	73
160	70	71
159	68	69
158	67	67
157	65	66
156	63	64
155	62	62
154	60	61
153	59	59
152	57	58
151	55	56
150	54	54
149	52	53
148	51	51
147	49	50
146	48	48
145	46	47
144	45	45
143	43	44
142	42	42
141	41	41
140	39	40
139	38	38
138	37	37
137	35	36
136	34	34
135	33	33
134	32	32
133	30	31
132	29	29
131	28	28
130	27	27
129	26	26
128	25	25
127	24	24
126	23	23
125	22	22
124	21	21
123	20	20
122	19	19
121	18	18
120	0	17

SECTION I

1.	C	8.	E	15.	C	22.	D
2.	B	9.	E	16.	C	23.	A
3.	A	10.	B	17.	A	24.	C
4.	C	11.	D	18.	D	25.	D
5.	A	12.	C	19.	A		
6.	D	13.	D	20.	B		
7.	A	14.	C	21.	B		

SECTION II

1.	B	8.	A	15.	E	22.	E
2.	E	9.	D	16.	A	23.	A
3.	C	10.	A	17.	C	24.	B
4.	C	11.	C	18.	B	25.	C
5.	D	12.	E	19.	D	26.	B
6.	C	13.	C	20.	B	27.	A
7.	C	14.	A	21.	B		

SECTION III

1.	B	8.	D	15.	B	22.	C
2.	D	9.	B	16.	E	23.	E
3.	E	10.	A	17.	C	24.	D
4.	C	11.	C	18.	E	25.	D
5.	D	12.	E	19.	D		
6.	A	13.	B	20.	C		
7.	A	14.	B	21.	B		

SECTION IV

1.	E	8.	A	15.	B	22.	D
2.	B	9.	B	16.	E	23.	C
3.	C	10.	E	17.	A	24.	E
4.	C	11.	E	18.	C		
5.	E	12.	B	19.	A		
6.	C	13.	D	20.	D		
7.	C	14.	D	21.	C		

On the following pages, you will find answers and explanations for all the questions that appear in the PrepTest on pages 11-38. Each question has been assigned a level of difficulty.

■ Level of Difficulty

The difficulty categories are based on test takers' responses to actual test items over several years. In each item type, the range of values covered by the actual items for "percentage correct"—that is, the percentage of test takers who answered an item correctly—was divided into five subranges. An item discussed here that falls into the easiest of these five (that is, was answered correctly by the highest number of test takers) is classified as "easy." Items in the next difficulty category are classified as "relatively easy," then "medium difficulty," "difficult," and "very difficult."

■ Organization

The explanations are divided into sets of questions corresponding to the sections of the test itself. They appear here in the same order as they appear on the PrepTest. Page numbers corresponding to the passage or question under discussion are highlighted in italics.

Logical Reasoning: Questions 1-25

Question 1 *(page 11)*

General Description: This question asks you to draw an inference based on the information presented. It is not enough that a response be true, if the information in that response is irrelevant to the information presented. Nor is it sufficient that a response present information that is merely consistent with the information presented in the passage; the best answer must present information that is supported by the information in the passage.

A. **Incorrect**. Since the passage does not say anything about adult sea turtles, or about the location of the adults, this claim is not supported by information in the passage.

B. **Incorrect**. The passage does not provide any information about the relation between ocean currents and the magnetic field of the Earth, and so this response is not correct.

C. **Correct**. Though the passage does not draw the conclusion that baby sea turtles can sense the magnetic field, the fact that the hatchlings change their direction certainly suggests that the hatchlings are responding to changes in the magnetic field. And if the hatchlings respond to the changes, then one reasonable inference is that they are able to sense the magnetic field. So, this is the best answer.

D. **Incorrect**. The information in the passage about the behavior of sea turtle hatchlings in the wild deals only with their behavior as they leave their hatching grounds. It provides no support for a claim about the sea turtles' behavior after they have left their hatching grounds.

E. **Incorrect**. The passage does not provide any information that would justify an inference about the behavior of hatchlings on the coast of Africa.

■ *Difficulty Level: Easy*

■ *Tips and Pitfalls: Read questions carefully. If a question asks which statement is supported by the passage, do not choose a response just because it seems on independent grounds to be plausible or likely—you must pick a response based on the information given in the passage.*

Question 2 *(page 11)*

General Description: This question asks you to identify the logical problem in an argument caused by failure to consider a logically relevant possibility. The best answer, then, will not merely present some possibility the argument fails to consider. Rather, it will be something the argument *should* have considered: a possibility that, if it turned out to be true, would tend to undermine the reasoning leading to the argument's conclusion.

A. **Incorrect**. It would not make the argument flawed to have ignored this possibility: the argument's conclusion is consistent with the possibility that the *other* half of Springhill's population has never been to Europe at all. Because the conclusion is consistent with this possibility, the argument does not *need* to address it.

B. **Correct**. If there were no overlap between the travelers to Italy and the travelers to France, then the argument's premises would provide good evidence for its conclusion: 20 percent + 30 percent = 50 percent. But the argument has presented no reason to suppose that there is no such overlap, and to the extent that there is, the argument is undermined. That is, if some people are counted both in the Italy group and in the France group, then the two groups together do not add up to 50 percent. (B) describes just this problem and is the best answer.

C. **Incorrect**. Far from ignoring this possibility, the argument seems to be assuming that it is actual. In fact, the greater the number of people from Springhill who have been to Italy or to France in the last five years, but not to both, the stronger the argument.

D. **Incorrect**. Far from ignoring this possibility, the argument seems to be assuming that it is actual. For if there were people from Springhill who had been to other European countries in the last five years, the argument would be stronger for mentioning them.

E. **Incorrect**. The argument is not faulty in ignoring this possibility, because it is irrelevant: The argument is about numbers of people who have been to Italy and/or France (and thus Europe) *at least* once in the last five years.

■ *Difficulty Level: Easy*

■ *Tips and Pitfalls: Though answering LSAT questions does not require performing any mathematical calculations, the questions do assume a college-level understanding of concepts that may be termed "mathematical," including "percent."*

Question 3 *(page 11)*

General Description: Since the question asks you to determine a point of disagreement between McBride and Leggett, the best answer will be the one describing a point that McBride accepts and Leggett rejects—or vice versa.

A. **Correct.** McBride opposes the introduction of fuel-efficiency standards precisely because these standards will discourage the manufacture of full-size cars, calling that prospect "troubling." So McBride would disagree with (A). Leggett, on the other hand, explicitly disagrees with McBride's position, arguing that the standards ought to be supported precisely because they discourage the manufacture of full-size cars and thus agreeing with (A). Thus, (A) is the best answer.

B. **Incorrect.** Though McBride and Leggett disagree about whether the standards should be implemented, both clearly are interested in the issue of safety, and it is quite plausible that one or both believe that fuel conservation is less important than is safety. However, this can be the best answer only if there is evidence that either Leggett or McBride believes that fuel conservation is not less important than is safety; the passage, however, provides no grounds for such an inference.

C. **Incorrect.** The passage does not provide enough information to judge whether McBride and Leggett disagree on this point. McBride's comments suggest agreement with it, but it is not clear where Leggett stands on the claim in question. Leggett says only that it is more likely that someone will be seriously injured in a collision if one of the cars is full-size, without specifying the location of the injured person.

D. **Incorrect.** Neither Leggett nor McBride mentions anything about the frequency of accidents; both are more concerned with the likelihood of harm should an accident occur.

E. **Incorrect.** Both Leggett and McBride agree that the new fuel-efficiency standards will discourage automobile manufacturers from building full-size cars. However, it is not clear that either believes that the standards will encourage the manufacture of more subcompact cars (as opposed to some third kind of car). Further, even if it is true that the reduction in full-size cars causes an increase in the manufacture of subcompact cars, this is a point of agreement, not disagreement, between Leggett and McBride. Of those who answered this question incorrectly, the majority chose (E), perhaps confusing the issue of whether manufacturers should be encouraged to build more subcompact cars with the issue of whether they will be encouraged to do so.

■ *Difficulty Level: Difficult*

■ *Tips and Pitfalls: When asked to determine a point on which two speakers are committed to agreement or disagreement, be sure to narrow your focus to explicit assertions by the speakers; avoid the temptation to speculate about what (else) either speaker might believe.*

Question 4 *(page 11)*

General Description: This question asks you to find the description of the strategy used by Leggett in arguing against McBride.

A.   **Incorrect**. McBride's and Leggett's conclusions contradict one another, but there is no suggestion that McBride's statements themselves contradict one another.

B.   **Incorrect**. Though the discussion focuses only on full-size and subcompact cars, neither party is presuming that all cars are either full-size or subcompact.

C.   **Correct**. From McBride's perspective, discouraging the manufacture of full-size cars is a bad thing, because McBride is considering the relative safety of a collision of two full-size cars and a "mixed" collision involving one full-size and one subcompact car. Leggett is shifting the perspective: Instead of comparing a mixed collision to a collision of two full-size cars, Leggett compares a two-car collision involving a full-size car to a collision of two subcompact cars. From that perspective, discouraging the manufacture of full-size cars is a good thing, because a collision of two subcompact cars is safer than a collision involving a full-size car. The two agree that the new fuel-efficiency standards will discourage the manufacture of full-size cars, but take different perspectives on the implication of that for automobile safety—and so reach opposite conclusions about whether the new standards should be supported.

D.   **Incorrect**. Leggett is raising doubts only about the conclusion McBride draws from the evidence, and that conclusion is "The new fuel-efficiency standards should therefore be opposed," which is not a generalization. This was the most popular incorrect answer.

E.   **Incorrect**. The "course of action advocated by McBride" is to oppose the new fuel-efficiency standards. Leggett is simply arguing in favor of supporting them, not claiming that it is impossible to take McBride's course.

■ *Difficulty Level: Difficult*

■ *Tips and Pitfalls: In answering questions about "argumentative strategy," it is imperative that you understand the structure of the argument in question. You also need to be able to compare the strategies described in the responses to the argument structure in the passage: If the response's strategy cannot be mapped exactly onto the argument structure, that response is not the best answer.*

Question 5 *(page 12)*

General Description: This question asks you to determine which one of the responses must be true, given the information in the passage. This is a very strong requirement. It may be easier to think of the task as determining which choice cannot be false, if the statements in the passage are true. Then you can rule out any choice that could be false.

A. **Correct**. Since the passage tells us that all degradable plastics are potentially useful packaging materials, and also that some degradable plastics leave residues of unknown toxicity, it is necessarily true that some potentially useful packaging materials (namely, those degradable plastics) leave residues of unknown toxicity. This is the best answer.

B. **Incorrect**. Though it is possible that some plastics would need both sunlight and submersion in order to decompose, the passage merely states that at least one is necessary. So, contrary to (B) it is quite possible that only sunlight or submersion is needed, and thus it is quite possible that (B) is false.

C. **Incorrect**. The passage focuses solely on the status of degradable plastics. However, it is quite possible that there are some other materials—that is, nonplastic materials—that need sunlight to break down. If there are no such materials, of course, the response need not be true. But even if there are, the passage gives no information about the status of these materials—they might or might not be potentially useful packaging materials. So in any case, (C) need not be true.

D. **Incorrect**. The passage says that some degradable plastics leave residues of unknown toxicity, but it does not say whether any substances other than degradable plastics leave such residues. For all we know from the passage, those degradable plastics are the only materials that leave such residues. Consequently, it is quite possible that all materials that leave residues of unknown toxicity are degradable plastics, and thus it is possible for this statement to be false.

E. **Incorrect**. This choice certainly is perfectly consistent with the information in the passage, and thus it certainly may be true. But it may be instead that these residues are left not by plastics that need to be buried in soil to break down, but rather only by the plastics that require submersion in water or exposure to sunlight to break down. Thus, it is possible for this statement to be false.

■ *Difficulty Level: Relatively easy*

■ *Tips and Pitfalls: Keep in mind that what "must be true" cannot be false and vice versa; in different questions and with different responses, conceiving of the question in one of these ways or the other may be easier for you. It is also worth repeating that "must be true" (as well as "cannot be false") is a very strong requirement: nothing that merely might be true, could be true, or even is quite likely to be true will be the best answer.*

Question 6 *(page 12)*

General Description: To answer this question, you must first recognize exactly what *is* the main conclusion of the argument. Then you should be able to consider how the argument goes about supporting that conclusion. You also need to be able to compare the methods of support described in the responses to the argument in the passage: if the response's method does not correspond exactly to that used in the argument, that response is not the best answer.

A. **Incorrect**. The number of experts on each side does not arise; rather, qualities of the experts on each side are discussed.

B. **Incorrect**. The idea of risks and consequences does arise in the argument, which may account for the popularity of this incorrect answer (chosen by the vast majority of those test takers who answered this question incorrectly). But the risks and consequences discussed are risks and consequences for the experts themselves, not for the people who may or may not believe those experts.

C. **Incorrect**. The economic prospects for investment *companies* are not mentioned at all. Further, though economic prospects for employees of such companies arise indirectly, even these prospects are not "projected" onto the economy as a whole.

D. **Correct**. The argument points out that the economists who support its conclusion are those who risk their jobs in making forecasts. If one group of experts is risking their jobs in making certain forecasts, that group has a *prima facie* reason to be more careful in making such forecasts than does a group of experts not risking their jobs in making such forecasts. This, the argument suggests, is a reason to think that the first group of experts is more reliable than the second, and thus a reason to believe the forecast made by the first group, namely, that the coming economic recovery will be strong. So (D) is the best answer.

E. **Incorrect**. It is too strong to call this argument an "attack" on anyone's "character": the argument simply points out facts about the two groups of experts.

■ *Difficulty Level: Difficult*

■ *Tips and Pitfalls: Keep in mind that for a response to be the best answer, it is not sufficient that it be connected to the passage in some way or other; it must relate in the specific way stated in the question.*

Question 7 *(page 12)*

General Description: The passage is suggesting that the information provided by the investment companies' economists is more trustworthy than the information provided by academic economists. So, a claim that weakens the argument would be one that weakens the trustworthiness of the information from the investment company's economists (or a claim that increases the trustworthiness of the academic economists).

A. **Correct**. If the interests of the economist's employer are likely to affect the economist's predictions as much as do more objective factors, this provides a reason to doubt the predictions. The predictions still might be accurate, depending on what exactly the interests of the employer are, but on the face of it, response (A)'s truth tends to weaken the argument in favor of taking the investment companies' economists more seriously than the academic economists. Thus (A) is the best answer.

B. **Incorrect**. At best, this choice is irrelevant to the conclusion of the argument; at worst, this choice supports the conclusion by giving a reason the forecasts of investment company economists should be taken more seriously.

C. **Incorrect**. This is a tempting choice, because one might reason that if the investment company economists include factors that make their methods problematic, and the academics don't, then their use of these methods would lead one to doubt the accuracy of the predictions made by the investment company economists. However, it is equally possible that including other factors improves the methods used by the investment company economists, and so this response has as much chance of supporting the argument as of weakening it.

D. **Incorrect**. Response (D) indicates a way in which the investment companies benefit from the accuracy of their economists' forecasts. This in turn provides a reason for the investment companies' economists to try to make their forecasts accurate, and thus, if anything, tends to strengthen the argument.

E. **Incorrect**. The passage says that the investment company economists are making predictions opposite from those made by academic economists. So if (E) is true, it provides support for the reliability of the investment company economists. Thus, far from weakening the argument, (E) would (if true) provide support for the argument.

■ *Difficulty Level: Relatively easy*

■ *Tips and Pitfalls: Be careful not to read more into a response than is actually stated. See, for example, (C).*

Question 8 *(page 13)*

General Description: This question asks you to identify the reasoning flaw in a given argument. For a response to be the best answer, it is necessary, but *not* sufficient, that it accurately describe some part of the argument: it must describe a feature of the argument in virtue of which the argument's reasoning is flawed.

A. **Incorrect**. John's desire to win the Mayfield raffle is mentioned, but not as part of what the argument says will increase the likelihood of his winning it.

B. **Incorrect**. The "activity itself" is entering the Mayfield (or any other) raffle. The "goal for which [John] pursues that activity" is to win the prize. There is no suggestion that the argument is confusing these two things.

C. **Incorrect**. The argument is not assuming, or even claiming, that John will be successful (i.e., will win the Mayfield raffle). The argument is about what will increase his chances of being successful.

D. **Incorrect**. The argument makes no claims that any event "cannot possibly occur." The argument is about what makes certain events more or less likely.

E. **Correct**. The phrase in this response "the likelihood that at least one event in a set of events will occur" refers to the passage's phrase "the likelihood of his winning one of them [i.e., the raffles]," if John enters raffles in addition to the Mayfield raffle. The passage goes on to refer to "*this* greater likelihood of winning *the Mayfield prize*" (emphasis added), which is response (E)'s "the likelihood that a designated event in that set will occur." To equate these two is to make a logical mistake: the first likelihood is the likelihood of John's winning some raffle or other, not that of his winning any particular raffle. That is, entering other raffles does not increase the chances of its being the Mayfield one that he wins; to think that it does is the flaw in the argument's reasoning.

■ *Difficulty Level: Relatively easy*

■ *Tips and Pitfalls: A general or abstract response is not necessarily better than a concrete, specific one.*

Question 9 *(page 13)*

General Description: This question asks you to determine whether Mary's actions are consistent with the actions and situations dictated by the principle. Answering this question requires precision: the elements of the situations and the actions dictated by the principle must match the response exactly if the principle in the passage is to apply correctly to a response.

A. **Incorrect**. The principle requires (among other things) that, when the stranger does not provide proof of being a government official, householders should not reveal information about their neighbors. The stranger merely claimed to be a detective, and a private detective at that, so—according to the principle—Mary should have either evaded the questions or refused to answer them; she did neither.

B. **Incorrect**. The stranger showed Mary a police badge, which counts as proof of being a government official. Still, there was no evidence that the stranger was on police business, and so—according to the principle—Mary ought to have refused to answer or evaded the questions. However, rather than refusing or evading, Mary lied, and lying is not an action supported by the principle.

C. **Incorrect**. The principle requires (among other things) that, when the stranger does not provide proof of being a government official, householders should not reveal information about their neighbors. The confused couple offered no such proof, and hence—according to the principle—Mary should have either evaded the questions or refused to answer them.

D. **Incorrect**. The strangers showed Mary valid identification as proof of being government officials, and also stated they were on official business. According to the principle, Mary ought to have answered their questions truthfully, but she instead gave an evasive answer.

E. **Correct**. The woman merely claimed to be an insurance adjuster, but did not offer any proof of being a government official. According to the principle, Mary was correct in politely evading her questions: this is the best answer.

■ *Difficulty Level: Relatively easy*

■ *Tips and Pitfalls: Questions that ask you to apply or interpret a principle require that you pay close attention to the exact limits of the principle. In particular, do not make assumptions about what would follow in some case outside the limits of what the principle actually addresses or includes.*

Question 10 *(page 14)*

General Description: This question asks you to find the response that can be inferred from the given passage. A statement that may well be true, but that is irrelevant to the passage, cannot be the best answer. Even a response that presents information consistent with the passage need not be the best answer. Rather, the passage must provide grounds or support for inferring the response in order for that response to be the best answer.

A. **Incorrect**. The passage does not consider how widely the scores range in either sport.

B. **Correct**. The passage says that in scoring competitive diving, the highest and lowest marks are discarded "in order to eliminate the possibility of bias." The passage concludes by saying that the "approach taken in diving. . . is a fairer system" than that used in scoring competitive figure skating. From these statements it can be inferred that with the current scoring systems, there is more chance of bias in scoring competitive figure skating than in scoring competitive diving, which is what (B) says. Thus (B) is the best answer.

C. **Incorrect**. In fact, the passage supports the opposite conclusion.

D. **Incorrect**. The passage says it is the discarding of high and low scores that is relevant to fairness, not the range of possible scores.

E. **Incorrect**. For all we know from the passage, there may be other facts about the scoring of competitive diving and figure skating such that diving would be no more vulnerable to bias than figure skating even if the discarding of high and low scores were eliminated. The passage compares the fairness of just one aspect of the sports, namely, their scoring processes. This was the most popular incorrect answer.

■ *Difficulty Level:* **Relatively easy**

■ *Tips and Pitfalls:* Do not infer merely from the fact that a passage focuses on one aspect of a phenomenon that there cannot be other relevant aspects.

Question 11 *(page 14)*

General Description: To answer this question, you must first recognize the pattern or structure of the reasoning in Rose's argument. Then choose the response whose argument is most like it in pattern or structure.

■ *Difficulty Level: Relatively easy*

■ *Tips and Pitfalls: When answering questions about "pattern of reasoning," look at the form of the argument, not its content. The fact that the argument in the passage is about authors and publishing is irrelevant to the question of its pattern of reasoning.*

A. **Incorrect**. The first step in this argument is similar to that in Rose's argument: it limits the possibilities to two. But the next step is different: instead of pointing out a property that each of the possibilities usually has, it makes a claim about a larger group, of which the two possibilities are members.

B. **Incorrect**. There are (at least) two ways in which the pattern of reasoning in this argument is different from that in Rose's argument. First, the second step here reasons to what must be the case for each possibility (i.e., "they must have opened Isidore's creaking gate"), whereas Rose reasons to what is generally the case (i.e., "Deerson's books are generally published by Quince Press, as are Jones's"). Second, unlike in Rose's argument, the final conclusion in response (B) introduces a new factor: the premises make no mention of what Isidore heard.

C. **Incorrect**. The first step in this argument, like that in Rose's argument, presents two possibilities. But the second step is different from that in Rose's argument: the second step here reasons to what is the case for each possibility (i.e., "Both these attributes are unsuitable in a customs inspector"), whereas Rose reasons to what is generally the case (i.e., "Deerson's books are generally published by Quince Press, as are Jones's"). Furthermore, the conclusion in response (C) is prescriptive ("George should not be hired. . ."), whereas Rose's conclusion is probabilistic ("the book is probably. . .").

D. **Correct**. The claim that Margarethe was born either in Luppingshavn or in Kindelberg parallels Rose's claim that the book was written either by Deerson or by Jones. The claim that most people in each city were of Mondarian descent parallels Rose's claim that both authors are generally published by Quince Press. The conclusion, that Margarethe probably had Mondarian ancestors, parallels Rose's conclusion that the book is probably published by Quince.

E. **Incorrect**. The pattern of reasoning in the first two steps of this argument is similar to that in Rose's argument. However, this argument uses evidence about what people say to support a conclusion about what is probably the case; Rose does not use evidence about what people say.

Question 12 *(page 14)*

General Description: This question asks you to determine the error of reasoning committed by the argument.

A.   **Incorrect**. It is not clear that, in saying that Sarah lied or that she cannot be trusted, the argument is attacking Sarah's character (as opposed to simply stating facts). But even if one does construe these statements as attacks on Sarah's character, response (A) is incorrect in saying that "[the argument] fails to offer any grounds" for these statements: the fact that Sarah lied about Emmett's haircut is presented as grounds.

B.   **Incorrect**. The argument does not confuse claims about the past with claims about the future. The argument makes claims about Sarah's past and implicit claims about the future ("Sarah cannot be trusted. . ."), but there is no suggestion that these are ever confused.

C.   **Correct**. The argument states that Sarah is "an excellent mechanic." Having lied about her opinion about a haircut is not clearly relevant to whether Sarah can be trusted to give an honest opinion about the mechanical condition of a car—the "sweeping claim" made by the argument. This is especially so, since the opinion whose honesty is in question is in an area in which Sarah is acknowledged to be an expert.

D.   **Incorrect**. A case could perhaps be made that the evidence in the argument is presented in "value-laden terms." But even if that were established, this response would still be incorrect, because the evidence presented does not presuppose the argument's conclusion.

E.   **Incorrect**. From the argument, the only kind of thing about which we can say Sarah may be a competent judge is mechanics (she is an "excellent mechanic"). The only other area in which her judgment arises here is her opinion of Emmett's haircut. But the argument makes no claims about Sarah's competence to judge haircuts. This was the most popular incorrect response.

■ *Difficulty Level: Medium difficulty*

■ *Tips and Pitfalls: Pay careful attention to the location of words with logical force, such as "not." For example, "not clearly relevant" means something quite different from "clearly not relevant."*

Question 13 *(page 15)*

General Description: This question asks you to determine which statement strengthens the argument that pink pterodactyls existed. The argument draws an analogy between pterodactyls and modern flamingos, and suggests that pterodactyls could have acquired a pink coloration in the same way that flamingos do: namely, by eating shrimp that get the pigment from red algae. So a statement that increases the likelihood that pterodactyls ate similar shrimp would strengthen the argument.

A.   **Incorrect**. If anything, this statement weakens the argument, since no evidence is presented that the relevant shrimp live or have ever lived in fresh water.

B.   **Incorrect**. This information is largely irrelevant to the argument, since the existence of this type of shrimp does not imply anything about the relation between these shrimp and the pterodactyls.

C.   **Incorrect**. This statement simply points out that if the pterodactyl did not eat a diet containing red algae, then its color—whatever that color may have been—was determined by something else. If the pterodactyl did not eat a diet containing red algae, then the analogy (and thus the argument) is weakened.

D.   **Correct**. If it is indeed the case that the habitat of the pterodactyl was rich in red algae and shrimp, then this increases the likelihood that, like the flamingo, the pterodactyl consumed the algae and shrimp. Thus, this choice strengthens the argument by increasing the probability that, like the flamingo, the pterodactyl took on a pink color.

E.   **Incorrect**. This choice discusses the status of modern day flamingos, and as such is largely irrelevant to the argument.

■ *Difficulty Level: Easy*

■ *Tips and Pitfalls: An argument by analogy is strengthened by additional points of similarity between the entities said to be analogous; it is weakened by points of dissimilarity.*

Question 14 *(page 15)*

General Description: This question asks you to resolve an apparent discrepancy in information. The discrepancy arises because the passage presents two pieces of information that are in conflict.

A. **Incorrect**. Statistical information about the percentage of drivers who use headlights for daytime driving in jurisdictions where such use is optional does not help to explain why making the use of headlights mandatory does not reduce overall collisions.

B. **Incorrect**. Rather than helping to resolve the apparent discrepancy, this statement would, if true, rule out a possible resolution. If, contrary to response (B), such a law were difficult to enforce, that might help explain why such laws do not reduce collision rates.

C. **Correct**. If only very careful drivers use headlights when their use is not legally required, then this explains why, when headlight use is optional, those drivers are less likely to be involved in a collision than are drivers who use headlights only when visibility is poor. It stands to reason that if headlight use is made mandatory, many less-careful drivers will also use headlights. But then the group of drivers using headlights expands to include not only the very careful drivers, but drivers of all sorts—including some who are not very careful. So it is not at all surprising that the overall number of collisions is not reduced: unsafe drivers do not become more careful when forced to use headlights.

D. **Incorrect**. This choice can do nothing to explain discrepancies between cases in which the use of headlights is optional when visibility is good and cases where the use of headlights is mandatory at all times. This choice introduces a third scenario that does not explain anything about either of the situations discussed in the passage.

E. **Incorrect**. If it is true that the jurisdictions in which the use of headlights is mandatory are areas that have poor daytime visibility, one might expect the use of headlights to reduce the overall number of collisions, at least in those places. But in any case, response (E) does not explain why, in jurisdictions where use of headlights is optional, drivers who use headlights at all times are less likely to be involved in collisions. This was the most popular incorrect answer.

■ *Difficulty Level: Difficult*

■ *Tips and Pitfalls: In answering a question about resolving the discrepancy between two pieces of information, remember that the best answer must explain both pieces of information. An answer that explains only one of the pieces of information is a tempting choice, but cannot be the best answer to a question that asks you to resolve a discrepancy.*

Question 15 *(page 15)*

General Description: This question asks you to determine the flaw in the argument's reasoning. In this question, each choice is phrased very generally. So, in order to answer the question, you must determine which general statement fits the argument's flaw.

A. **Incorrect.** The argument does present "one possible solution to a problem," but it does not exclude the possibility of other solutions to the problem. This was the most popular incorrect answer.

B. **Incorrect.** The argument relies on a standard use of "inefficient"; there is nothing ambiguous in that usage.

C. **Correct.** Even if it is true that requiring industries to pay full price for water would reduce waste, the claim that "inefficient use...would soon cease altogether" is far too strong. The evidence presented does suggest that forcing industries to pay full price for the water they use might reduce water waste somewhat. But the argument has not ruled out the possibility that even if industries paid full price for their water, it would still be more expensive for industries to prevent the waste entirely than to pay for the wasted water—that is, that industries would still waste some water. So the argument's reasoning is flawed in that it draws a conclusion stronger than what is warranted by its evidence.

D. **Incorrect.** The argument presumes that there is some connection between the cost of water and industries' propensity to waste it, but it does not assume the precise connection made in the conclusion.

E. **Incorrect.** All the evidence presented is relevant to the argument's conclusion.

■ *Difficulty Level: Difficult*

■ *Tips and Pitfalls: A general response must fit exactly if it is to be the correct response; responses that are partly accurate (for example, [A] in this case) in describing the argument cannot be correct.*

Question 16 *(page 16)*

General Description: This question asks you to find the assumption required by the argument. In other words, find the statement whose truth is required if the argument is to succeed in demonstrating its conclusion.

A. **Incorrect.** How much of the funding each founder provides is not at issue.

B. **Incorrect.** Though it is consistent with the argument that some founding members can provide both funding and skills, the argument does not need to assume this. It is also quite consistent with the argument that no founders offer both funding and skills. This was the most popular incorrect response.

C. **Correct.** If new companies were not more likely to succeed in the way described in response (C), then the argument would not be justified in drawing its conclusion. That is, suppose a new company were just as likely, or more likely, to succeed while securing funding and skills from nonfounders as from founders. In that case, the fact that single individuals are unlikely to be able to offer both funding and skills would not be evidence that companies founded by groups are more likely to succeed than companies founded by individuals, for in that case, the individual founder could get funding and/or skills from nonfounders without thereby lowering the chances of the company's succeeding.

D. **Incorrect.** The argument does not make or rely on any assumptions about how easy it is to acquire different business skills.

E. **Incorrect.** This may well be true, but the argument need not assume that it is true; the argument can support its conclusion just as well if it turns out that response (E) is false. The important contrast in the argument is between people who provide funding and people who provide any of the relevant skills. The different combinations of skills people may bring are not at issue.

■ *Difficulty Level: Medium difficulty*

■ *Tips and Pitfalls: Another way to think about the question of whether an assumption is required by an argument is to think about what happens to the argument if the assumption turns out to be false. If the argument cannot possibly succeed when the assumption is false, then the assumption is required by the argument.*

Question 17 *(page 16)*

General Description: This question requires you to determine which response is most supported by the information given. In answering this sort of question, look for the choice that has the firmest grounding in the claims made in the argument.

A. Correct. The information presented shows a relationship among rotting logs, the red-backed vole, and the fungi and fungi-spores. The spores in turn develop into fungi that "assist the trees" in various ways. Thus the presence of rotting logs can have beneficial effects on the trees around them.

B. Incorrect. The information indicates that the red-backed vole subsists almost entirely on the portion of certain specialized fungi that grows aboveground. There is no indication that the vole is able to derive nutrients from the spores if it does eat them.

C. Incorrect. There is no indication that the trees would not survive without the voles to distribute the spores.

D. Incorrect. The passage indicates that the fungi-spores are deposited on the forest floor, but nothing in the passage indicates that the spores must be deposited near the roots of trees in order for the spores to survive.

E. Incorrect. The passage does not suggest that the dead and decaying trees are the environment in which the fungi grows. The rotting trees provide a habitat for the voles.

■ *Difficulty Level: Relatively easy*

■ *Tips and Pitfalls: In answering this sort of question, be careful not to choose a response that is stronger than what is supported by the passage (for example, response [C]).*

Question 18 *(page 16)*

General Description: This question asks you to determine a point at issue between the two speakers. The task, then, is a matter of determining which of the choices is a claim supported by one speaker but rejected by the other.

A. Incorrect. Mayor Tyler says that the courthouse "is costing" the city $30 million "to build." This indicates that the courthouse is being built, and nothing in Councillor Simón's claims indicates a rejection of this point.

B. Incorrect. Councillor Simón explicitly advocates this claim. However, nothing in what Mayor Tyler says indicates whether Mayor Tyler accepts or rejects this claim. Response (B) was the most popular incorrect response.

C. Incorrect. Councillor Simón refers to "your own financial reports," and thus clearly attributes them to Mayor Tyler. Mayor Tyler, however, never rejects this claim, and so there is no dispute between Tyler and Simón on this point. Further, Councillor Simón's claim does not explicitly address whether the financial reports attributed to Mayor Tyler are "major" financial reports.

D. Correct. Mayor Tyler says that in 1982 the courthouse would "relieve the overcrowding we were experiencing"; Tyler clearly believes that the courthouse was needed in 1982. Tyler also believes it is needed in 1992, referring to the courthouse as "the courthouse that Roseville still needs." Councillor Simón, on the other hand, explicitly rejects this point, saying that building the courthouse in 1992 meant that Roseville saved money by "not having to maintain an *underutilized* courthouse for ten years." (emphasis added)

E. Incorrect. Neither Councillor Simón nor Mayor Tyler gives a specific amount for the cost of maintaining the courthouse for the period between 1982 and 1992.

■ *Difficulty Level: Difficult*

■ *Tips and Pitfalls: In a "point of disagreement" question, a choice that presents a claim that is supported or denied by one speaker, but about which the other speaker has made no commitment either way, cannot be correct. In other words, for a response to be the correct response, it is not sufficient that the speakers might disagree about it. Limit your analysis to what is actually said; avoid the temptation to speculate about what (else) either speaker might believe.*

Question 19 *(page 16)*

General Description: The conclusion of Mayor Tyler's argument is that the city would have saved money if the courthouse had been built in 1982 rather than in 1992. Thus, you must pick the response that provides support for this claim.

(A.) Correct. This response describes an expense that the city incurred before the courthouse was built, an expense that (the response says) could have been avoided had the courthouse been built in 1982. Thus it adds support to Tyler's conclusion that the city would have saved money if the courthouse had been built in 1982.

B. Incorrect. Information about the number of court cases does not directly imply anything about the cost of the courthouse.

C. Incorrect. Even if the mayor's proposal to build a courthouse was met with greater opposition in 1982 than in 1992, this is irrelevant to the claim that building the courthouse in 1982 would have saved money.

D. Incorrect. A proposal submitted by Councillor Simón in 1980 is not relevant to the mayor's argument, which is an argument about the comparative costs of building the courthouse in 1982 and in 1992. Hence, this claim, even if true, could not support the mayor's conclusion.

E. Incorrect. This statement cannot support the mayor's conclusion, because it is irrelevant: crowded prison conditions do not bear on the mayor's conclusion about the costs associated with building the courthouse.

■ *Difficulty Level: Relatively easy*

■ *Tips and Pitfalls: Since this question asks what would support Mayor Tyler's conclusion, Councillor Simón's part of the passage can safely be ignored in answering it.*

Question 20 *(page 17)*

General Description: This question asks you to find an assumption made by the reasoning. In other words, find the statement whose truth is required if the conclusion is to be successfully defended.

A. Incorrect. The conclusion can still be proven without assuming that each and every one of the 70 professional opera companies is a commercially viable operation, so long as most of them are viable.

(B.) Correct. If (B) is false, that means that 45 or more professional opera companies were active 30 years ago and have since ceased operations. In that case, though 45 of the currently active companies were founded over the last 30 years, during that same period 45 or more other companies ceased operations. Thus, over the last 30 years, there would have been at best no change in the total number of professional opera companies, or perhaps even a reduction in that number. So if (B) is false, there are no grounds for drawing a conclusion about an "explosion" of public interest in opera from the evidence presented in the passage. Thus (B) is the best answer.

C. Incorrect. The passage makes no claims about the relative popularity of opera and other performing arts, and so does not have to make an assumption of this sort.

D. Incorrect. An increase in the size of the average audience need not be assumed; an alternative is that there are many more performances now than 30 years ago, and so the total audience has increased.

E. Incorrect. The conclusion can still be proven without assuming that each and every one of the 45 most recently founded opera companies was established as a result of enthusiasm on the part of a potential audience. Further, for all we know from the passage, founding an opera company may well generate the kind of enthusiasm described in the conclusion, in which case the founding of new opera companies would be evidence for the conclusion even if (E) is false. Response (E) was by far the most popular incorrect response.

■ *Difficulty Level: Very difficult*

■ *Tips and Pitfalls: Another way to think about the question of whether an assumption is required by an argument is to think about what happens to the argument if the assumption turns out to be false. If the argument cannot possibly succeed when the assumption is false, then the assumption is required by the argument.*

Question 21 (*page 17*)

General Description: This question asks you to determine which response most strengthens the argument. In approaching such questions, you should identify the conclusion of the argument, and find the response that, if true, adds to the argument's support for its conclusion.

A. **Incorrect.** In discussing the literary qualities of the broadsides, this choice offers information that is largely irrelevant to the argument.

B. **Correct.** The argument's conclusion is that the existence of many broadsides that are "moralizing in nature" does not provide evidence that most seventeenth-century people were serious about moral values. Response (B) strengthens the argument by showing that the moralizing aspect of the broadsides was rather minimal, and by providing a possible alternative reason for the popularity of broadsides.

C. **Incorrect.** This response is at best irrelevant to the argument, and at worst, weakens it. Buying printed sermons would seem on the face of it to be evidence of seriousness about moral values.

D. **Incorrect.** The clergy's interest in moral values (as evidenced by their warnings about strong drink) does not support the conclusion drawn in the argument—that the moralizing broadsides do not provide evidence that most seventeenth-century people were serious about moral values.

E. **Incorrect.** The attitude of the well-educated people of the time toward broadsides and broadside peddlers is irrelevant to the argument in the passage.

■ *Difficulty Level: Medium difficulty*

■ *Tips and Pitfalls: It may seem obvious to say that if the question asks for strengthening evidence, one should not choose weakening evidence, and vice versa, but this is an easy mistake to make, especially when answering questions quickly.*

Question 22 (*page 17*)

General Description: This question asks you to find the assumption necessary to the argument. In other words, find the statement whose truth is required if the argument is to succeed in demonstrating its conclusion.

A. **Incorrect.** The argument does not need to assume that most character flaws are considered trivial by those who have them. The argument deals only with the flaws that people admit to having. It leaves open the possibility that most character flaws are neither admitted to nor considered to be trivial by those who have them.

B. **Incorrect.** The argument considers character flaws that an individual considers trivial, but there is no indication in the argument that the opinion of other people is relevant to an individual's assessment of whether a particular character flaw is trivial or serious.

C. **Incorrect.** It is consistent with the argument that, rather than confessing to flaws only when they must, individuals admit to having trivial character flaws rather freely.

D. **Correct.** Suppose people sometimes readily admit to having a character flaw even when doing so causes them psychological discomfort (i.e., that [D] is false). In that case, from the first sentence of the passage it follows that people sometimes readily admit even to character flaws they do not consider trivial. That is, if (D) is false, then a person's admitting to a certain character flaw would not show that the person considered that flaw to be trivial; in short, the argument's conclusion would not follow. Thus (D) is the best answer.

E. **Incorrect.** The argument considers only the individual's own assessment of character flaws, and thus does not need to assume anything about how others perceive these flaws.

■ *Difficulty Level: Medium difficulty*

■ *Tips and Pitfalls: Another way to think about the question of whether an assumption is required by an argument is to think about what happens to the argument if the assumption turns out to be false. If the argument cannot possibly succeed when the assumption is false, then the assumption is required by the argument.*

Question 23 *(page 17)*

General Description: In looking for the response that most helps to explain the situation presented in the passage, first try to understand the situation. Then decide what it is about that situation that might need to be explained.

A. **Correct.** The most straightforward travel plans would involve a series of weekly round-trip tickets for flights departing on Tuesday and returning on Friday. But, excluding the trip that departs on the first Tuesday of the semester and returns the last Friday, Popkin's request is for a series of flights that leave on Friday and return on Tuesday. This response gives an explanation of why she would choose this travel arrangement over the more straightforward approach—namely, that if the round-trips are scheduled over Saturdays, then she saves money.

B. **Incorrect.** This suggests that Popkin's instructions will make her tickets more expensive than the apparently more straightforward travel plans involving a series of weekly round-trip tickets for flights departing on Tuesday and returning on Friday. Thus, it alone makes her behavior more mysterious, not less.

C. **Incorrect.** In the situation described in the passage, Popkin does not take any more round-trips, nor does she complete round-trips any sooner, than she would with more straightforward travel plans involving a series of weekly round-trip tickets for flights departing on Tuesday and returning on Friday.

D. **Incorrect.** Since the passage does not say anything about Popkin's payment arrangements for the trips, this choice cannot explain anything about her instructions to her travel agent.

E. **Incorrect.** The passage does not say anything about Popkin's payment arrangements for the trips, and therefore this choice does not explain anything about her instructions to her travel agent.

▪ *Difficulty Level: Very difficult*

▪ *Tips and Pitfalls: Much of the work in answering this question comes in figuring out what exactly needs explaining in Professor Popkin's instructions. There is no explicit discrepancy, as there is in other questions of this sort.*

Question 24 *(page 18)*

General Description: This question asks you to find the response that contains an error in reasoning similar to that contained in the passage's argument. To do this, you must understand the error in the passage's argument. Then choose the response that exhibits the most similar error.

A. **Incorrect.** In this response, the argument explicitly asserts the similarity of "many occasions" to the "present" occasion. That is, unlike the argument in the passage, this argument presents evidence that the specific case is not unusual.

B. **Incorrect.** This argument does not appear to have an error of reasoning. Even if one were to argue that it does have an error, though, it could not be the error in the passage, since the argument in (B) makes no use of a specific case to draw a conclusion about a more general situation.

C. **Correct.** The error of reasoning in this choice is similar to the error of reasoning in the passage. The error in the passage is the argument's failure to recognize that a specific case—the last week of the theater's operation—is unusual in a relevant way and thus might not represent the general situation. Likewise, the argument in (C) assumes that what is true of a small group of students is also true of a much larger group, without recognizing that the smaller group might be unusual in a relevant way: namely, they were interested enough to come to the meeting.

D. **Incorrect.** This argument may perhaps be criticized for presuming a certain theory of fairness (namely, that fairness is a matter of equal percentage reductions) without providing any evidence to support that presumption. But there is no use of a specific case to draw a conclusion about a more general situation, so this argument's error would still not be similar to that in the passage.

E. **Incorrect.** This argument may be criticized for drawing an inference about the library's budget based on information about the budget of the athletic department without establishing the relevance of that information. But there is no use of a specific case to draw a conclusion about a more general situation, so this argument's error would still not be similar to that in the passage.

▪ *Difficulty Level: Difficult*

▪ *Tips and Pitfalls: When asked to find a similar reasoning error, it is often helpful to look at the passage and responses from a formal point of view; the fact that the passage is about a drive-in movie theater is irrelevant to the question of the error in reasoning.*

Question 25 *(page 18)*

General Description: This question asks you to find the assumption on which the argument relies. In other words, find the statement whose truth is required if the argument is to succeed in demonstrating its conclusion.

A. **Incorrect.** The argument compares the costs of making glass bottles from recycled glass and from raw materials. An assumption about the relative costs of plastic bottles and glass bottles is not necessary for the argument as presented.

B. **Incorrect.** The argument does not have to assume that recycled glass can account for a large percentage of the glass bottles made by soft drink distributors. The conclusion is only that by using recycled glass, bottlers can reduce costs: The argument does not make any claims about the degree to which costs can be lowered.

C. **Incorrect.** The argument does not have to make an assumption about the consumer's ability to distinguish between bottles made from recycled glass and bottles made from raw materials. Such an assumption is (without additional assumptions) irrelevant to the argument about costs.

D. **Correct.** For the claim that bottlers would lower costs by using recycled glass to be successfully defended, the argument must assume that no additional costs are associated with the process of making new bottles from recycled glass, such that the savings would be negated. This response says that a plausible cost of that sort in fact does not negate the savings. Thus, it is the best answer.

E. **Incorrect.** The argument does not need to assume that there are fewer steps involved in the process of making molten glass from recycled glass than in the process of making molten glass from raw materials. Insofar as the argument considers the comparative costs of the processes, the number of steps involved is not directly relevant without additional assumptions.

■ *Difficulty Level: Very difficult*

■ *Tips and Pitfalls: Another way to think about the question of whether an assumption is relied upon by an argument is to think about what happens to the argument if the assumption turns out to be false. If the argument cannot possibly succeed when the assumption is false, then the argument relies on the assumption. Also, be careful not to speculate about what other situations might be implied by a given response (for example, speculating that lower cost must mean fewer steps).*

Reading Comprehension: Questions 1-27

Passage (*page 19*): The most important thing to keep in mind as you read this passage is that the author describes the positions of two different scholars in it, and then evaluates the work of the two scholars in the last paragraph. In the first paragraph, the author describes the work of the historian Philippe Ariès, who argued that medieval Europeans did not view childhood as a distinct period of development. The author then describes the work of Shulamith Shahar, who attempts to show that childhood *was* seen as a distinct period of development in medieval Europe. Finally, in the last paragraph the author states that Shahar's work is successful in undermining Ariès' claim regarding the medieval European view of childhood, but that her work falls short as a rebuttal to Ariès' work in general. According to the author, Ariès' more central point is that the family as a private and powerful institution organized around children is a relatively modern ideal; but, the author says, Shahar fails to address this point. Keeping the views of the scholars and the author distinct in your mind is absolutely essential for answering the questions correctly.

General strategy for answering questions: Be sure that you read all five responses before selecting your answer. Some responses may seem right when considered alone. But when you read the correct response, it should become clear that it is the best answer and that the other responses only *seem* right.

1. **This question (*page 19*) asks you to identify the author's purpose in writing the passage.**

A. **Incorrect**. Shahar's work challenges Ariès' traditional theory, but neither Shahar nor the author of the passage is dismissive of Ariès' work. In fact, the author of the passage is even somewhat critical of Shahar's work, judging it to be "uncomfortably incomplete" (line 49) as a rebuttal to the traditional theory.

B. **Correct**. This is the best answer because it most accurately expresses the author's purpose in writing the passage: The passage focuses on Shahar's recent research, first describing her work and then evaluating it with respect to the existing work of Philippe Ariès.

C. **Incorrect**. Because the two opposing theories of medieval childhood considered in the passage are never reconciled, this response can be ruled out.

D. **Incorrect**. The primary purpose of the passage is not to refute Shahar's main arguments but to discuss and assess her attempt to refute Ariès' arguments.

E. **Incorrect**. It is not clear what the unusual phenomenon might be, but insofar as information is summarized at all in the passage, such summary is offered only in the course of the passage's presentation and evaluation of the two scholars' competing arguments about medieval concepts of childhood.

■ *Difficulty Level: Difficult*

2. **This question** (*page 19*) **asks you to distinguish between the statement that is supported by the passage and those that are not.**

A. **Incorrect**. This response misconstrues the statement in lines 22-26 of the passage, which says that medieval accounts of saints' lives emphasize the saints' personal piety. In contrast, (A) says that medieval accounts of childhood *in general* emphasize the piety of their subjects.

B. **Incorrect**. While it is true that the passage describes medieval stories regarding saints' miracles as especially significant (lines 26-29), the passage does not say that medieval accounts of saints' lives focus on these miracles *rather than* on the saints' childhoods. Instead, the passage maintains that the accounts of saints' lives are informative on both counts.

C. **Incorrect**. Lines 20-22 reveal that Shahar "makes intelligent use of medical writing and theological works." In other words, such works are an important source of the evidence Shahar marshals in support of her argument, yet (C) says these sources provide scant evidence.

D. **Incorrect**. This response misstates the comparison in lines 4-9.

E. **Correct**. This is the best answer because it paraphrases what the passage says in lines 4-9: that children in medieval text illustrations are distinguished from adults by their smaller stature rather than by a distinctively childlike appearance.

■ *Difficulty Level:* *Medium difficulty*

3. **This question** (*page 20*) **asks you to identify the rhetorical function of a single paragraph within the context of the passage.**

A. **Incorrect**. The evidence mentioned in the first paragraph is evidence that Ariès himself offered in support of his theory, not evidence that he failed to take into account. Evidence that Ariès presumably fails to take into account is mentioned in subsequent paragraphs only.

B. **Incorrect**. The only "historical sources" to which this paragraph refers—medieval text illustrations—are not the focus of the debate between Ariès and Shahar. There is no indication anywhere in the passage that Shahar's work even considers medieval text illustrations.

C. **Correct**. This response most completely and accurately expresses the function of the first paragraph in the context of the passage: The first paragraph provides a brief summary of the traditional argument (Ariès') that Shahar's recent research, as it is described in the rest of the passage, challenges.

D. **Incorrect**. There is no "puzzling historical phenomenon" described in the first paragraph. The passage as a whole attempts not to account for a specific historical phenomenon but to describe opposing arguments made by two historians about the same topic—the medieval view of childhood.

E. **Incorrect**. The only "important information" about the Middle Ages referred to in the first paragraph is that which Ariès cited in support of his argument. While the paragraph does refer to certain historical facts, its function in the passage is not to "summarize information" about that period.

■ *Difficulty Level:* *Easy*

4. This question *(page 20)* asks you to identify the author's intent in bringing up a particular piece of evidence.

A. **Incorrect**. This option is not correct because the author brings up the evidence in question as part of an explanation of how Shahar undermines Ariès' hypothesis about childhood in medieval Europe, not as part of a comparison between perceptions of childhood during and after the Middle Ages. In fact, the author does not seek to make such a comparison anywhere in the passage; the author merely discusses the arguments of Ariès and Shahar concerning how perceptions of childhood may or may not have changed. The author offers the particular piece of evidence in question in order to show how Shahar supports her views.

B. **Incorrect**. This option is incorrect because the author states that Shahar used the evidence regarding apprenticeships to conclude that the parents in question were *conforming* to social norms (lines 43-47) which presumes that Shahar was indeed aware of those norms.

C. **Correct**. The information regarding the apprenticeship of children between the ages of 7 and 11 plays a central role in Shahar's argument that childhood was viewed as a distinct stage in human development in medieval Europe. As lines 43-47 indicate, Shahar concludes on the basis of this evidence that parents saw apprenticeships as a way to secure children a niche in society, a goal that indicates both particular concern for children and a belief that special measures had to be taken to secure such niches for children.

D. **Incorrect**. This option fails because while the issues of class and, indirectly, gender do come up, they are only tangentially connected to the author's purpose in mentioning the apprenticeship of boys aged 7 to 11. The author brings up the question of how boys of the wealthier classes were treated in order to make a broader point. This distinction is a rather subtle one, and not surprisingly, most of the test takers who got this question wrong picked (D).

E. **Incorrect**. The third paragraph and the passage as a whole say little directly about the role of children in the family. And regarding the medieval conception of childhood *per se*, the information in the third paragraph helps to establish that, in Shahar's view, it was similar to the modern conception, despite Ariès' claim to the contrary.

■ *Difficulty Level: Medium difficulty*

5. This question *(page 20)* asks you to evaluate the effect of additional evidence on Shahar's claims.

A. **Incorrect**. According to the passage (lines 26-29), accounts of miracles performed by saints on behalf of infants and children provide significant support for Shahar's argument that children were the focus of adult care and concern in the Middle Ages.

B. **Incorrect**. This response furnishes fairly strong support for Shahar's arguments, specifically for her claim that people in the Middle Ages viewed childhood as a distinct developmental phase during which the young should undergo "training...in stages" to prepare them to assume the roles and responsibilities of adulthood.

C. **Incorrect**. This response represents additional evidence in support of Shahar's assertion that the actions of medieval parents did, in fact, demonstrate concern for children.

D. **Correct**. This response represents a challenge to Shahar's argument. Shahar relies on the assumption that medieval accounts of saints' lives can be read as providing reliable "evidence of parental concern for children." If the accounts in question do not actually reflect the attitudes of parents in the Middle Ages, then Shahar would have to find other, more reliable evidence to support her claims about parental attitudes.

E. **Incorrect**. This response provides further evidence that concern for children was expected of parents— at least among the wealthier classes—in the Middle Ages. It supports Shahar's claim that "it was a social norm to ensure one's children a future niche in society."

■ *Difficulty Level: Relatively easy*

6. This question *(page 20)* asks you to move beyond what the passage states explicitly by inferring which of the five responses makes a statement with which Ariès would not be likely to agree.

A. **Incorrect**. Ariès would be likely to agree with this statement because it corresponds closely to a view attributed to him in lines 9-13 of the passage: "Ariès also suggested that high infant mortality rates in the Middle Ages induced indifference toward offspring as a defense mechanism...."

B. **Incorrect**. Ariès would be likely to agree with this statement because the passage states that the ideal of the family as a powerful, private institution is a relatively modern one, "whose origins Ariès related to the growing influence of the middle classes in the postmedieval period" (lines 56-58).

C. **Correct**. This is the correct response because it contradicts lines 53-56 of the passage: "But central to Ariès' position was the contention that the family as a powerful and private institution organized around children *is a relatively modern ideal...*" (italics added). Given this statement, it is clear that Ariès would not agree that the ideal of the family as a powerful and private institution developed in the Middle Ages.

D. **Incorrect**. We can infer that Ariès would be likely to agree with this statement because Ariès used medieval text illustrations as evidence of people's views of childhood in medieval Europe, and in these illustrations "the children look like miniature adults" (lines 8-9).

E. **Incorrect**. That Ariès would be likely to agree with this statement is clear from lines 54-56: "...the family as a powerful and private institution organized around children *is a relatively modern ideal...*" (italics added).

▪ *Difficulty Level: Relatively easy*

▪ *Note: To answer this question, you have to keep in mind that this question concerns Ariès' views only, and that the views of Shahar and the author are irrelevant here. Also, remember that the correct response will be the only one with which Ariès would probably not agree.*

7. This question *(page 20)* asks you to distinguish between issues that are addressed in the argument the passage describes and issues that are not.

A. **Incorrect**. The question of whether parents in the Middle Ages felt affection for their children is one of the central questions to which Shahar's work, as it is described in the passage, is addressed. Part of her project is to counter Ariès' argument about parental indifference toward children by providing documentary evidence that parents in the Middle Ages did, in fact, feel and show concern for their children regardless of the high infant mortality rate.

B. **Incorrect**. The answer to this question about the influence of social norms can be found at the end of the third paragraph, where the passage states that "Shahar concludes that parents placed their children in monasteries or as apprentices...because it was a social norm to ensure one's children a future niche in society."

C. **Correct**. This is the only one of the five questions to which Shahar's work does not provide an answer according to the passage. The passage makes no mention of a change in the perception of the family *during* the Middle Ages—according to Ariès, the change took place in the postmedieval period. More important, the passage says that Shahar does not even comment on this postmedieval change in the perception of the family.

D. **Incorrect**. The answer to this question about a particular stage of childhood can be found at the beginning of the third paragraph, which refers to Shahar's discussion of specific parenting practices during "the period in childhood from ages 7 to 11."

E. **Incorrect**. According to the passage (lines 50-52), Shahar's work "succeeds in demonstrating that people in the Middle Ages did view childhood as a definite stage in human development... ."

▪ *Difficulty Level: Medium difficulty*

8. **This question** *(page 20)* **asks you to make an inference regarding the author's view of Shahar's research in relation to Ariès' theories about childhood in the Middle Ages.**

A. **Correct**. This is the correct response because it can be inferred by putting together several of the author's statements from the last paragraph. In the second sentence of this paragraph, the author indicates that Shahar's work successfully undermines Ariès' argument that childhood was not viewed as a distinct stage in human development in the Middle Ages (lines 50-53). Nonetheless, in the previous sentence the author had stated that Shahar's work is "uncomfortably incomplete" as a rebuttal to Ariès (lines 48-49). Lines 54-58 identify a contention that is central to Ariès' position (the modern ideal of the family as a powerful, private institution), and the author ends the passage by stating that Shahar does not comment on these issues (lines 61-62). Thus, the author would agree that while Shahar's work challenges certain of Ariès' arguments, it does not refute his central position.

B. **Incorrect**. The author believes that although Shahar's work does not refute Ariès' central position, it does show one of Ariès' important views to be incorrect (lines 50-53). Thus the author would not be likely to agree that Shahar's work provides no new information.

C. **Incorrect**. The author states that Shahar does not comment on the larger issues that make up Ariès' central point (lines 61-62). Thus the author would not be likely to agree that Shahar's research refutes Ariès' central position.

D. **Incorrect**. While the author allows that Shahar's research refutes one of Ariès' arguments (lines 50-53), there is nothing in the passage to indicate that Shahar confirms any of Ariès' arguments. In fact, the first sentence of the last paragraph suggests that the author sees Shahar's work as an effort to rebut Ariès' overall position.

E. **Incorrect**. The author mentions medieval infant mortality rates as a piece of evidence used by Ariès (line 10). Nowhere are infant mortality rates mentioned in connection with Shahar's work. Thus the author would not be likely to agree that Shahar's work provides more information on this topic than Ariès' work did.

■ *Difficulty Level: Relatively easy*

Passage *(page 21)*: This passage begins with a brief explanation of the phenomenon of greenhouse warming, goes on to explain the scientific controversy over the exact dimensions of the problem, and concludes by making a specific policy recommendation. It is important to note that while the passage cites discrepant evidence and describes the differing views of scientists, the author does not actually "take sides" in the scientific debate over greenhouse warming. Instead, the author proposes pursuing a course of action that responds to the potential severity of the problem without presupposing that the most dire scientific predictions will necessarily come true. This "no regrets" policy is described in the last paragraph as a policy of immediate, moderate action—one that defers more costly measures until the scientific data are sufficiently conclusive to determine whether such measures will, in fact, be necessary.

General strategy for answering questions: Be sure to read each response completely before choosing an answer, because some incorrect responses may actually be partially correct. Also, be mindful of whose views or opinions are being described at various points in the passage; not every view expressed in the passage can be attributed to the author.

9. **This question *(page 21)* asks you to identify the main idea of the passage.**

A. **Incorrect**. While the "no regrets" policy advocated in the passage does encourage government agencies to implement affordable measures to combat the possible effects of global warming, there is no indication in the passage that the author believes such measures are likely to be ineffective.

B. **Incorrect**. This response contradicts lines 51-52 of the passage, which state that the "wisest policy" in light of current scientific uncertainty about rising global temperatures "is not to forestall action."

C. **Incorrect**. The level of certainty reflected in this response is inconsistent with the passage's repeated assertions that scientists disagree concerning whether greenhouse gases have caused a rise in global temperatures and to what extent, if any, they might do so in the future. In light of this disagreement, the author recommends that costly measures be deferred until more conclusive information about greenhouse warming becomes available.

D. **Correct**. This response both acknowledges the current lack of consensus in the scientific community concerning the problem of greenhouse warming and concisely summarizes the "no regrets" policy that the author advocates in the final paragraph.

E. **Incorrect**. The passage makes no claims at all concerning the relationship between environmental policies implemented by politicians now and scientists' ability to make accurate predictions in the future about the progress of global warming.

■ *Difficulty Level: Easy*

10. **This question** *(page 21)* **asks you to draw an inference based on information provided in the passage**.

A. **Correct**. Lines 32-34 of the passage suggest that the rise in global temperatures could be caused by one of two factors: a natural fluctuation in temperatures or the increase in greenhouse gases.

B. **Incorrect**. According to the first paragraph, greenhouse warming occurs when heat from the sun warms the Earth and is prevented from being reradiated into outer space. Based on this information, one would expect that an increase in solar reradiation might contribute to a *drop*, not a rise in global temperature.

C. **Incorrect**. According to the passage, a 20 percent *increase* in levels of atmospheric carbon dioxide over the last century could be causing global temperatures to rise. By analogy, one would expect that a 20 percent decrease in these levels over the next half century could cause global temperatures to fall.

D. **Incorrect**. Line 2 of the passage identifies "other trace gases" besides atmospheric carbon dioxide as possible contributors to greenhouse warming. We can infer based on this information that a decrease in atmospheric levels of such gases would probably not lead to a rise in global temperature. If anything, such a decrease would be more likely to lead to a drop in global temperature.

E. **Incorrect**. In the passage, the author asserts that the replacement of fossil-fuel energy with solar energy "make[s] sense for economic or environmental reasons *besides* greenhouse warming" (lines 52-54). Given this qualification, the passage does not provide sufficient information to support a valid inference about what impact this step could have on global temperatures. But to the extent that the passage suggests anything at all on this matter, it suggests that replacing fossil-fuel energy with solar energy might help prevent, or at least slow down, a global warming trend.

■ *Difficulty Level: Medium difficulty*

11. **This question** *(page 21)* **asks you to identify the organizational structure of the passage**.

A. **Incorrect**. While the passage does describe a scientific problem (greenhouse warming) and, ultimately, recommend a course of action, it does not evaluate discrepancies among proposed solutions. The discrepancies presented in the passage are not among proposed solutions but among ways of understanding the nature of the problem.

B. **Incorrect**. The author does not make a case for any given side in the dispute over greenhouse warming and doesn't explore the political repercussions of any given side's position. The passage is neutral in its description of the debate over the causes and effects of global warming.

C. **Correct**. This response most completely and accurately reflects the organization of the passage: The phenomenon of increasing levels of atmospheric carbon dioxide is described in the first paragraph; different views of the effects of this phenomenon are presented in the second and third paragraphs; and a policy of "no regrets" is proposed in the last paragraph as a way of responding pragmatically to these different views.

D. **Incorrect**. This response can be ruled out because the passage never offers a solution to the "scientific puzzle" of greenhouse warming. Instead, the author recommends a course of action for policymakers to pursue in light of the fact that important scientific questions concerning greenhouse warming remain unanswered. Insofar as the "no regrets" policy itself can be construed as a solution, it is one that addresses the problem of how to proceed in the *absence* of a solution to the "scientific puzzle" of greenhouse warming.

E. **Incorrect**. The passage doesn't explain any "generally accepted scientific formula," nor does it examine a case that violates the principle on which the putative formula is based, so this response is inaccurate on both counts.

■ *Difficulty Level: Medium difficulty*

12. This question (*page 22*) asks you to identify the purpose of a specific reference made by the author of the passage.

A. **Incorrect**. The author of the passage emphasizes the fact that there is currently no conclusive evidence by means of which to resolve the differing scientific views concerning the question of greenhouse warming. The passage therefore offers no recommendation about how such differences can be resolved.

B. **Incorrect**. Although the author of the passage identifies natural climatic fluctuation as one possible explanation for the apparent rise in global temperatures over the past century, he or she doesn't argue anywhere in the passage that such fluctuation is the probable cause of this warming trend; therefore, the author would not have cited the meteorological data in question for the purpose of supporting such an argument.

C. **Incorrect**. The passage presents the 20 percent increase in carbon dioxide levels over the last century not as a "prevailing view" but as an established scientific fact (lines 7-10 and lines 18-19). What the passage identifies as "the prevailing view" (line 22-23) is an interpretation of the climatic record which maintains that global temperatures for the entire globe increased from 0.5 to 1.0 degree Fahrenheit over the past century.

D. **Incorrect**. There is little indication in the passage that the author believes that observation points outside of North America are inadequate. Moreover, in this part of the passage, the author is concerned with the question of how to evaluate existing evidence for global warming; he or she does not seek to make any suggestions for improving upon current methods of data collection.

E. **Correct**. The author asserts in lines 27-30 that data collected in North America "does not confirm" (in other words, casts doubt on) the conclusion that global temperatures have increased. The author cites these data to point out the difficulty of drawing clear conclusions about the extent of global warming.

■ *Difficulty Level: Medium difficulty*

13. This question (*page 22*) asks you to draw an inference about what the author would be likely to believe based on information provided in the passage.

A. **Incorrect**. The passage does not provide a basis for this inference because the author makes no claims at all concerning the relationship between the efficacy of measures that could be undertaken to reverse global warming and the cost of such measures. He or she simply recommends deferring costly measures until conclusive information about greenhouse warming becomes available to scientists.

B. **Incorrect**. According to the passage, costly measures to combat greenhouse warming should be taken (if they are necessary) when scientists have a clearer and more definitive understanding of the process of global warming. There is no support in the passage for inferring that the author would agree that this moment will have been reached "only when the rise in temperature begins to exceed human beings' capacity to adapt to such an increase."

C. **Correct**. The assertion made in this response is wholly consistent with the "no regrets" policy described in the last paragraph of the passage. The suggestion that less costly measures be implemented before expensive ones is implicit in the author's recommendation that "steps that make sense for economic or environmental reasons besides global warming" be implemented now and that "more costly measures" be reserved for a time when scientists have definite information about the process of greenhouse warming.

D. **Incorrect**. The passage does not suggest any causal connection between the adoption of a "no regrets" policy and the resolution of scientists' uncertainty concerning greenhouse warming. While the passage asserts that a "no regrets" policy should be implemented in anticipation of such a resolution, it does not suggest that adopting the policy will in any way hasten the resolution.

E. **Incorrect**. This response considerably exaggerates the author's position. While the author recommends that the measures undertaken *initially* should "make sense for economic or environmental reasons besides greenhouse warming," the passage does not suggest that *any* measure should be implemented *only* if it addresses other environmental problems.

■ *Difficulty Level: Medium difficulty*

14. **This question** *(page 22)* **asks you to draw an analogy between material that is presented in the passage and material that is similar but not directly related to the passage.**

A. **Correct**. The scenario and the course of action described in this response closely parallel the scenario described in the passage and the course of action recommended in the last paragraph. Like the "no regrets" policy described in the passage, the policy outlined in (A) involves undertaking modest measures in the face of uncertainty—"an inexpensive but scientifically valuable program"—in the near term, to be followed by "more costly measures [if they] are warranted."

B. **Incorrect**. This response involves the requisite case of scientific uncertainty, but the course of action it outlines does not resemble the two-stage, wait-and-see approach of the "no regrets" policy described in the passage. The approach suggested in (B) is an all-encompassing one which is implemented in spite of a lack of conclusive scientific information.

C. **Incorrect**. This response involves the requisite case of scientific uncertainty, but the course of action described here is unlike the "no regrets" policy in that it involves the direct implementation of a costly remedial program.

D. **Incorrect**. Although the "no regrets" policy recommends immediate action, it does so without accepting the position of any one scientific group. The author of the passage does not presuppose that the most dire predictions about global warming are going to come true and does not endorse a policy such as the one described here, which is predicated on the inevitability of such predictions.

E. **Incorrect**. This response offers the requisite scenario of scientific uncertainty, but the course of action it outlines does not resemble the two-stage, wait-and-see approach of the "no regrets" policy. The remedial action proposed in this option is in the form of "relatively inexpensive modifications" that will presumably meet the new building-code requirements. Another important difference is that the earthquake in the scenario is "highly probable, whereas" the likelihood of greenhouse warming is very uncertain.

■ *Difficulty Level: Difficult*

Passage *(page 23)*: This passage is particularly complex in that it discusses three competing interpretations of a particular historical phenomenon, namely, the opposition of nineteenth-century feminists to legislation aimed at restricting women's work hours. The first paragraph presents two competing interpretations of this phenomenon: the first of these is by liberal legal historians, the second by labor historians. The second paragraph introduces a third and more recent perspective on the issue—that of feminist historians. The last paragraph of the passage turns to the question of how protective labor legislation for women should be evaluated in general, with the author asserting that neither liberal legal historians nor labor historians offer a "fully adequate" analysis of the issue. Feminist historians, the author goes on to argue, stand to make a "major contribution" not only to our understanding of the history of women and labor legislation but also to our efforts to theorize the social impact of the law. In answering the questions that accompany this passage, it is very important to keep the three arguments presented in the passage clear in your mind.

15. **This question** *(page 23)* asks you to clarify the meaning of a particular phrase as it is used in the passage.

A. **Incorrect**. The passage is more concerned with the reception of a particular set of laws than it is with specific strategies for influencing the production of laws. Furthermore, the focus on social class is associated with labor historians in the passage, while the phrase "age of collectivism" is associated with liberal legal historians.

B. **Incorrect**. The focus on social class is associated with labor historians in the passage, but the phrase "age of collectivism" is associated with liberal legal historians. It would be more consistent with the liberal legal historians' position to infer that legislators during this time viewed workers in the wider context of society at large rather than in the relatively narrow context of social class.

C. **Incorrect**. The passage discusses the "age of collectivism" neither in terms of the competing interests of the various social classes nor in terms of the needs of the state. In the passage, class competition is a dynamic associated not with liberal legal historians, who use the phrase "age of collectivism," but with labor historians. Furthermore, the idea that the state is an abstract entity with needs of its own is completely external to both of the historical interpretations described in the first paragraph.

D. **Incorrect**. The passage is more concerned with the reception of laws than it is with the production of laws. And while the passage does discuss a particular element of society's legislative agenda in the "age of collectivism," it neither states nor implies anything relating to the overall scope of that agenda.

E. **Correct**. This response accurately paraphrases lines 6-11, which explain the "age of collectivism" in very broad philosophical terms as a time when the government shifted its emphasis from the rights of the individual to the welfare of society as a whole.

■ *Difficulty Level: Relatively easy*

16. **This question** *(page 23)* **requires you to apply general ideas from the passage to a question that is not directly addressed in the passage.**

A. **Correct**. This answer's characterization of legal historians' approach matches up very well with what we read regarding legal historians in the first paragraph: according to these historians, the nineteenth century was an "age of collectivism" because "an emphasis on welfare replaced the emphasis on individual rights" (lines 7-8). So legal historians would indeed represent protective labor laws as an outgrowth of a general shift in societal ideas from individual rights to welfare. The characterization of the labor historians' approach also matches the account in the first paragraph, where we read that labor historians see protective labor laws as the result of a struggle against injustices. They also accuse the feminists who opposed such laws as seeking equality between privileged men and women, all the while ignoring the need to rethink "the economic bases of social relations" (lines 22-28). Thus a labor historian's view would differ from that of a legal historian in that the labor historian would see the labor laws as the result of political struggles against an economically and socially privileged class.

B. **Incorrect**. It is incorrect to say that labor historians would dismiss the practical consequences of the laws for their supporters. The passage makes it quite clear that labor historians interpret these laws as a necessary tool for redressing socioeconomic injustices, a view which presupposes a belief that the laws had real beneficial effects.

C. **Incorrect**. The legal historians analyze the feminists' motives for opposing the labor laws, but there is no evidence that they approve of these motives. In fact, their attribution of the feminists' position to their *"single-minded* campaign for women's suffrage" (lines 16-17) (italics added) suggests that the legal historians disapprove of the feminists' priorities.

D. **Incorrect**. There is no indication in the passage that legal historians would dispute the existence of inequities in nineteenth-century British society. Indeed, the fact that they attempt to explain the enactment of protective labor laws for women and children suggests that they are well aware of inequities within that society and of efforts to alleviate them.

E. **Incorrect**. The fact that labor historians are critical of nineteenth-century feminists for failing to support the protective labor laws indicates that they believe that the laws had a positive impact on workers.

■ *Difficulty Level: Very difficult*

■ *Note: The right answer for a question like this one, which asks you to compare two approaches to a historical writing, must be accurate on both counts. Responses that are right about only one of the two cannot be correct, no matter how accurate they might seem to be regarding that one topic.*

17. **This question** (*page 24*) **asks you to identify a way in which proponents of one argument offer an implicit critique of a competing argument.**

A. **Incorrect**. The interpretation offered by feminist historians does not include any reference to enlightened members of the middle class who promoted protective labor legislation for women. In the feminist historians' argument, only the government and trade unions are cited as contributors to the enactment of such legislation. It would therefore not be reasonable to infer that the feminist historians would criticize labor historians for minimizing the contribution of an enlightened middle class.

B. **Incorrect**. The idea that there was a shift in the perception of the state's role prior to the passage of protective labor legislation is associated in the passage with neither feminist historians nor labor historians, but with liberal legal historians. It would not be reasonable to infer that feminist historians would criticize labor historians for ignoring a philosophical shift that doesn't figure in either group's interpretation of the phenomenon in question.

C. **Correct**. By examining the ways in which protective legislation actually hurt working-class women, feminist historians bring to light major disadvantages of protective labor legislation that were overlooked by labor historians. According to the first paragraph (lines 19-28), labor historians view feminist opposition to protective labor laws as the product of selfish middle-class women who sought to expand their own privileges at the expense of the working-class women (and men) who stood to benefit from such laws. Feminist historians respond to this argument by pointing out that women of all classes had good reason to mistrust such legislation, which was often designed not so much to protect women as to force them out of the workplace, thereby protecting the prerogatives of their husbands and the job security of working men (lines 32-41).

D. **Incorrect**. The argument about women's "single-minded" focus on obtaining the vote is attributed in the passage not to feminist historians or labor historians, but to liberal legal historians. Therefore, arguments about suffrage would not logically figure into feminist historians' critique of the views of labor historians.

E. **Incorrect**. The argument of the feminist historians does not address, even indirectly, the issue of the potential benefits of political equality for working-class women in the nineteenth century. Arguments concerning the question of political equality for women are associated in the passage with neither feminist historians nor labor historians, but with liberal legal historians. It is therefore not reasonable to infer that feminist historians would view the studies of labor historians as inadequate on the grounds that such studies underestimated the potential benefits of political equality for working-class women.

■ *Difficulty Level: Difficult*

18. **This question** *(page 24)* **asks you to move beyond the explicit content of the passage and draw an inference about the views of liberal legal historians.**

A. **Incorrect**. The passage provides no grounds for concluding that legal historians attribute British feminists' position to a worry that protective labor laws would not benefit anyone until they applied to all workers. Instead, the passage says that, according to legal historians, feminists worried that supporting the laws might conflict with the theoretical underpinnings of their support for women's suffrage.

B. **Correct**. According to legal historians, protective labor laws were an outgrowth of a shift in societal priorities from individual rights to collective welfare (lines 6-11). Legal historians also argue that feminists "could not afford to seem to favor these 'special' laws for women" because their efforts to gain suffrage for women relied heavily on "arguments derived from eighteenth-century theories of individual rights and equality" (lines 14-19). Taken together, these two assertions imply that British feminists were worried that supporting the protective labor laws would undermine their arguments in favor of women's suffrage, which were based on ideas about individual rights rather than collective welfare.

C. **Incorrect**. The passage does not imply that legal historians believe that feminists were unaware of the potential benefits of the laws for women. The passage indicates that, according to legal historians, feminists devoted themselves exclusively to a "single-minded" campaign for women's suffrage.

D. **Incorrect**. The passage provides no evidence for concluding that legal historians see the feminists' pursuit of suffrage as an effort to remedy other injustices against women quickly; in fact, legal historians' characterization of British feminists' campaign for suffrage as "single-minded" suggests that, in the historians' view at least, the feminists had no other objectives in mind. So while it may seem to be reasonable to make the connection between the vote and efforts to address exploitation, the passage does not give us a basis for concluding that legal historians attribute this strategy to feminists.

E. **Incorrect**. Legal historians say that British feminists worried that supporting protective labor laws might have negative consequences, but there are no grounds for inferring that legal historians think that feminists worried that the laws themselves, if enacted, would lead to other laws restricting women's rights. The legal historians' explanation deals only with the worries feminists had about the effects supporting protective labor laws might have on their efforts to win women's suffrage.

■ *Difficulty Level: Very difficult*

19. This question *(page 24)* asks you to derive the meaning of a term from the context in which the term is used.

A.   **Incorrect**. This is too indirect an inference to draw given the context. In the context of the last paragraph of the passage, the assertion that the analysis of labor historians is "class-based" is meant primarily to affirm that labor historians base their arguments on the concept of social class, not to suggest that they dismiss arguments based on other concepts.

B.   **Incorrect**. While the passage does describe labor historians as focusing on the issue of class in their analysis of protective labor legislation, it does not suggest that their analyses are politically partisan, limited only to those arguments that can be used to promote the interests of the working classes.

C.   **Incorrect**. The passage does not suggest that labor historians were willing to equate gender and class by viewing women as a social class unto themselves. On the contrary, labor historians' argument that women of the middle class sought to advance their own interests at the expense of their working-class counterparts (lines 24-28) suggests that labor historians view class affiliation as a more decisive factor than gender affiliation when it comes to assessing individuals' motivations and actions.

D.   **Correct**. This response is most consistent with the labor historians' approach to the issue of feminist resistance to protective labor laws. According to the passage, labor historians emphasize the fact that feminist opponents of protective labor laws belonged to the middle class. They further assert that these middle-class women had selfish political aspirations that were rooted in a collective sense of class privilege and in the desire to increase that privilege, even if it meant ignoring the injustices to which others were being subjected.

E.   **Incorrect**. This is too indirect an inference to draw given the context. The term "class-based" is used very broadly in the last paragraph to refer to a mode of historical analysis that focuses on the role of class allegiance in the decisions of individuals. Although labor historians might well assert that the working classes were oppressed by an unjust political and economic system, the term "class-based," as it is used in the last paragraph, does not strongly suggest such an assertion.

■ *Difficulty Level: Very difficult*

20. This question *(page 24)* requires you to identify which explanation is attributed by the passage to feminist historians.

A.   **Incorrect**. It is possible to conclude that legal historians or labor historians see the British feminists' position as inconsistent, but feminist historians argue that the British feminists had "plentiful reasons" (line 30) for opposing such laws. Far from being inconsistent with their support for women's suffrage, the feminists' opposition to the laws derived, according to the feminist historians, from their belief that the laws were not really intended to protect women's interests.

B.   **Correct**. The author states in the second paragraph that feminist historians see the British feminists' opposition as a response to male-dominated unions' support for legislation "aimed at forcibly excluding women from wage labor," (lines 38-39) either to preserve jobs for men or to maintain a husband's right to his wife's unpaid labor. An additional factor, according to the feminists, was the government's self-interested policies aimed alternately at enticing women into the labor market during labor shortages and pushing them out to open up jobs for men during job shortages.

C.   **Incorrect**. While it is true that, according to feminist historians, women trade unionists had few male allies within the trade-union movement, the passage provides no evidence that the British feminists opposed the protective labor laws in response to active requests from women trade unionists.

D.   **Incorrect**. This response implies that, in the eyes of nineteenth-century feminists, legislators might have had good intentions in proposing protective labor laws, but they simply did not realize that such laws would affect women negatively. In contrast to this view, feminist historians argue that nineteenth-century feminists believed that government policies were intended to serve the interests of men and of the government itself, often at the expense of women's interests.

E.   **Incorrect**. It is true that there was tension in the nineteenth century between male and female trade unionists, but it is an oversimplification to say that feminists opposed the protective labor laws simply because male trade unionists supported them. The feminists' opposition was based not on hostility toward male trade unionists, but rather on their perception of the intent and probable consequences of the laws.

■ *Difficulty Level: Difficult*

Passage *(page 25)*: This passage discusses a recent book titled *Black Writers in Latin America* by Richard L. Jackson, a literary critic who is interested in issues of race in Latin American literature. Unlike his previous volume, *The Black Image in Latin American Literature*, which had discussed attitudes toward black people as revealed in literature by Latin American authors with a variety of ethnic backgrounds, Jackson's new study focuses specifically on black experience as represented by African Hispanic authors. The author of the passage attributes this narrower focus to Jackson's view that "personal identification with blackness and personal experience with the black experience" are requisite for being able to represent the black experience authentically. According to the author, this view allies Jackson with other North American critics who view African Hispanic literature as distinct and "culturally autonomous," in contrast to critics who view African Hispanic literature through the lens of the Latin American ideal of "racial blending." In the last paragraph, the author offers a subtle criticism of Jackson's approach. He argues that some of the examples cited by Jackson, such as the poetry of African Hispanic writer Nicolás Guillén, actually undermine Jackson's argument in that they seem no more authentic than the work of non-black Hispanic contemporaries who represent black experience.

Overall, this is quite a difficult reading passage. The language is sophisticated, and the important positions are not stated or identified in any obvious way. To answer the questions correctly you must keep several features of the passage distinct in your mind: the differences between Jackson's two books, the differing views of the two groups of critics of Latin American literature, the author's response to Jackson's approach, and the role played by Nicolás Guillén in the author's argument.

21. **This question *(page 25)* asks you to distinguish what the passage says regarding Richard L. Jackson's previous study from what it does not say.**

A. **Incorrect**. The passage says of Jackson's previous study (titled *The Black Image in Latin American Literature*) that it looks at "the writings of both black and non-black authors" (lines 5-6). It is his latest study that discusses the black experience as represented in the work of black authors exclusively.

B. **Correct**. The passage says that Jackson's previous book "studied various attitudes toward black people in Latin America" (lines 9-11), and also that it "examined ethnic themes in the writings of both black and non-black authors" (lines 4-6).

C. **Incorrect**. This response closely mimics a statement made in the passage not about Jackson's earlier work, but about Jackson's most recent book: "the later work examines the black representation of black consciousness in Spanish American literature from the early nineteenth century to the present" (lines 12-14). There is no indication in the passage that Jackson's previous work examines literary texts spanning roughly two centuries.

D. **Incorrect**. The passage states that Jackson "joins a number of other North American critics" (line 23) in his approach to African American literature, but that is quite different from the claim that the North American conception of this literature is the focus of Jackson's book.

E. **Incorrect**. Like some other North American critics, Jackson believes that African Hispanic literature should be treated as culturally autonomous. According to the passage, an emphasis on integration can be found not in Jackson's work, but in the work of critics with whom Jackson disagrees.

■ *Difficulty Level: Medium difficulty*

22. This question *(page 25)* requires you to evaluate the impact of additional evidence on Jackson's position.

A. **Incorrect.** The characteristic that Jackson identifies as essential to an author's authentic representation of black experience in Latin America is "personal experience with the black experience" (line 17), not lifelong residence in Latin America. Thus, if Jackson supported his argument by citing novels by authors who turned out to have lived in the United States before they moved to Latin America, that in itself would not undermine his position.

B. **Incorrect.** Jackson's argument relies on an assessment of the works of Palés Matos, Ballagas, and other non-black Hispanic poets associated with the Negrista movement as superficial and inauthentic in their representations of black experience (see lines 53-59). Even if these authors are shown to have plagiarized the work of African Hispanic poets, Jackson's position is not undermined since plagiarizing works that are (presumably) authentic does not make the plagiarizers' works authentic. In fact, such plagiarism would seem to reinforce, rather than weaken, the claim that the Negrista works are inauthentic.

C. **Incorrect.** Jackson conceptualizes African Hispanic literature as "culturally autonomous" (line 25). If it is discovered that African Hispanic authors have usually developed by reading and imitating the works of other black authors, that would tend to strengthen, rather than undermine, Jackson's position.

D. **Incorrect.** It does not undermine Jackson's position to say that early-twentieth-century Hispanic authors "consider" racial integration since these authors are not necessarily African Hispanic. And even if they are African Hispanic, they might very well consider integration as an aspect of black experience, and they might consider it from a uniquely black perspective. Moreover, Jackson concedes that many African Hispanic authors actually espouse integration (lines 33-36); his emphasis on the centrality of ethnicity is independent of authors' views on integration.

E. **Correct.** According to the author, Jackson argues that "only black writers have the necessary insight and mastery of the appropriate techniques to depict their situation authentically" (lines 20-22). If it is discovered that some of the literary texts that Jackson offers as examples of authentic portraits of black experience were actually written by non-black poets, his claim that only black writers can represent black experience authentically would be invalidated.

■ *Difficulty Level: Very difficult*

23. This question *(page 25)* asks you to identify the option that most accurately describes the rhetorical and logical structure of the second paragraph.

A. **Correct.** The beginning of the second paragraph describes the point of view adopted by Jackson in his recent study; namely, that only black writers can represent black experience authentically and that African Hispanic literature is culturally autonomous. The author then places this view in a broader scholarly context by contrasting it with the view of critics who, influenced by the Latin American ideal of racial blending, argue that black and non-black writers in Latin America share the same cultural context.

B. **Incorrect.** The second paragraph does begin by stating Jackson's point of view, but there are no contradictory examples offered as evidence against Jackson's views.

C. **Incorrect.** The author does explain Jackson's point of view and then relate it to others in the second paragraph, but the author does not offer any critical evaluation of Jackson's point of view in this paragraph. Rather, the author criticizes Jackson's position in the third paragraph.

D. **Incorrect.** The second paragraph does begin by describing Jackson's point of view and comparing it to a competing view, but it does not attempt to reveal any assumption on which Jackson's views depend. More importantly, the author does not criticize Jackson's point of view in this paragraph.

E. **Incorrect.** The second paragraph does outline Jackson's point of view and juxtapose it with a competing view, but there is nothing in this paragraph that can be construed as an effort to show that Jackson's view lacks historical perspective.

■ *Difficulty Level: Difficult*

24. **This question** *(page 26)* **asks you to distinguish what the passage says regarding some of Nicolás Guillén's poems from the 1920s from what it does not say.**

A. **Incorrect**. The author says that some of Guillén's poems from the 1930s are no more authentic than similar poems by some non-black poets. But the author does not go so far as to say that any of Guillén's poems are *less realistic* than poems by non-black poets. In fact, the author suggests that Guillén's poems from the 1920s are particularly realistic in their depiction of social ills.

B. **Correct**. The option matches the author's statement that "several of Guillén's poems from the 1920s show an awareness of social ills like poverty, unemployment, and racial discrimination that is absent from the work of peers influenced by the Negrista movement" (lines 49-53).

C. **Incorrect**. In his book, Jackson argues that Guillén's "dramatic conversion to blackness" (lines 46-47) was a reaction against the Negrista movement, rather than a sign that he had joined it. In either case, the assumption is that the founding of the movement predated Guillén's reaction to it. In addition, the author compares poems by peers of Guillén's who were influenced by the Negrista movement unfavorably to Guillén's poems from the 1920s, which further suggests that Guillén did not belong to the movement.

D. **Incorrect**. While Jackson would probably argue that direct personal exposure to black experience was necessary for Guillén to be able to represent black life authentically, nowhere does the passage mention what Guillén's actual experiences were or how those experiences might have influenced his work.

E. **Incorrect**. The author compares some of Guillén's poems to those of Palés Matos and Ballagas, but there is no suggestion that these poets were influenced by Guillén in any way.

■ *Difficulty Level: Difficult*

25. **This question** *(page 26)* **asks you to move beyond what the passage states explicitly by inferring which of the five responses makes a statement with which the author of the passage would be likely to agree.**

A. **Incorrect**. While the author agrees with the first part of this response statement ("Validating only the representations of African Hispanic consciousness found in the works written by black writers is a flawed approach…"), the remainder of the response goes too far beyond the author's position. The author argues only that there is no reason to think that non-blacks are intrinsically incapable of representing black experience; there is no evidence that the author believes that many of the *most* convincing representations of *any* racial group are written by outsiders. The latter is a sweeping claim that is not supported by the passage.

B. **Incorrect**. It is Jackson who argues that, because of their experiences, African Hispanic writers are uniquely capable of representing black characters and experiences authentically. In the third paragraph, the author of the passage is critical of this view.

C. **Correct**. In considering the poetry of Nicolás Guillén, the author writes that his work from the 1920s shows an awareness of some of the social ills affecting African Hispanics that is missing from the work of his contemporaries (lines 49-53). This statement, and the rhetoric of concession with which it begins ("Admittedly…"), indicate that the author would agree that studying the work of Guillén as an African Hispanic writer could yield insights into African Hispanic experience that could not be derived from an examination of the work of his non-black contemporaries. On the other hand, it is clear from the overall argument in the third paragraph that the author disagrees with Jackson's contention that actually being African Hispanic is a necessary condition for being able to portray African Hispanic experience authentically.

D. **Incorrect**. While the author does not object explicitly to the fact that Jackson's new study focuses on the work of African Hispanic writers exclusively, there is no indication in the passage that the author would agree that the works of African Hispanic and non-black Hispanic authors *should* be considered separately. In fact, since the author does object to Jackson's motivation for focusing on the work of African Hispanic authors exclusively, there is some reason to think that the author might have a preference for treating the works of black and non-black authors together.

E. **Incorrect**. Nothing in the passage supports inferring that the author would agree with the statement in this response. In fact, since this statement seems to privilege the works of black authors over those of non-black authors as the standard of authenticity in representing African Hispanic experience, it is likely that the author would disagree with this response.

■ *Difficulty Level: Very difficult*

■ *Tips and Pitfalls: Of the test takers who got this question wrong, twice as many picked (B) as any other incorrect answer. Since (B) accurately describes one of Jackson's beliefs, it seems likely that many of these test takers misread the question as asking about Jackson's views rather than the author's. As always, it is extremely important to read the questions carefully and to keep the competing points of view in the passage straight in your mind.*

26. **This question** *(page 26)* **asks you to draw an analogy between material that is presented in the passage and material that is similar but not directly related to the passage.**

A. **Incorrect**. The North American approach to African Hispanic literature is based on the assumption that it is culturally autonomous, with styles and themes derived from African Hispanics' experiences of oppression. This approach thus looks exclusively to African Hispanic writers for authentic insights into African Hispanic identity. In contrast, the hypothetical study in this response focuses on paintings by both ethnic Hungarians and painters of other ethnic backgrounds as a way of understanding Hungarian identity.

B. **Correct**. Like the North American approach to African Hispanic literature, which focuses exclusively on African Hispanic writers as the authoritative chroniclers of black experience in Latin America, the hypothetical study in this response focuses exclusively on paintings by ethnic Hungarian artists in its analysis of Hungarian identity.

C. **Incorrect**. The hypothetical study in this response attempts to define Hungarian identity by focusing on the paintings by both Hungarians and non-Hungarians that are most popular with the Hungarian public. In contrast, the North American approach to African Hispanic literature focuses on literary texts written by African Hispanic authors without regard to whether they are popular with the African Hispanic public.

D. **Incorrect**. The North American approach to African Hispanic literature is based on the assumption that having had experiences that are unique to one ethnic group is what determines the authenticity of a writer's attempt to represent that group. In contrast, the hypothetical study in this response attempts to understand Hungarian art by showing how it conforms to worldwide artistic movements.

E. **Incorrect**. While the North American approach to African Hispanic literature is interested in African Hispanic writers primarily for their representations of specifically black experiences in Latin America, the hypothetical study in this response looks for representations of universal human concerns in paintings by ethnic Hungarians.

■ *Difficulty Level: Very difficult*

27. **This question** *(page 26)* **asks you to identify the main idea of the passage.**

A. **Correct**. The author identifies a central feature of Jackson's approach to African Hispanic literature—his focus on African Hispanic writers on the assumption that only they can represent African Hispanic experience authentically—and points out that this feature is shared by a number of other North American critics. The author then proceeds to argue that this feature is flawed. The author contends that several poems offered by Jackson as examples of authentic African Hispanic writing are in fact as superficial as similar works by non-black poets.

B. **Incorrect**. The author does point to a significant flaw in Jackson's argument, but nowhere does he or she say that Jackson relies on the Latin American perspective of racial blending and integration. In fact, the passage says that Jackson sees African Hispanic literature as culturally autonomous.

C. **Incorrect**. The author does not criticize Jackson on the ground that the authors, poets, and texts he chooses are not representative of Spanish American literature in general. In fact, the question of whether these writers are representative of a broader Spanish American literary tradition is irrelevant to the passage.

D. **Incorrect**. The author notes that the focus of Jackson's new study signals a shift in the emphasis of his work, but the primary focus in the passage is on Jackson's approach in his new study, not on the implications of this approach for his previous work.

E. **Incorrect**. Jackson's views on Guillén play a subordinate role in the passage, not a central role: they are cited as evidence of the flaws inherent in Jackson's approach. Moreover, far from attempting to integrate African Hispanic writers into worldwide literary movements, Jackson argues that African Hispanic literature in general, and Guillén's work in particular, should be distanced from non-black literature.

■ *Difficulty Level: Very difficult*

Logical Reasoning: Questions 1-25

Question 1 (*page 27*)

General Description: This question requires you to identify the issue over which the historian and the city council member disagree.

A. **Incorrect**. Both the historian ("it became a great city") and the city council member ("Megapolis' past glory") believe that Megapolis was once a great city.

B. **Correct**. The historian gives an explanation of how Megapolis became a great city: it was "administered wisely, with vision and with universal public support." The city council member responds with "Not so," and goes on to give a different explanation of Megapolis' greatness. This is the best answer.

C. **Incorrect**. Neither the historian nor the city council member takes a stand on this general issue.

D. **Incorrect**. The historian makes a statement to this effect, but it is never denied by the city council member.

E. **Incorrect**. The current status of Megapolis is not discussed.

▪ *Difficulty Level: Easy*

▪ *Tips and Pitfalls: In a "point of disagreement" question, a choice that presents a claim that is supported or denied by one speaker, but about which the other speaker has made no commitment either way, cannot be correct. In other words, for a response to be correct, it is not sufficient that the speakers might disagree about it. Limit your analysis to what is actually said; avoid the temptation to speculate about what (else) either speaker might believe.*

Question 2 (*page 27*)

General Description: This question asks you to draw a logical inference from the information given in the passage.

A. **Incorrect**. While this statement may be true, the passage provides no support for it. On the contrary, the passage is about great architects, who (according to the passage) do *not* exhibit "a slavish lack of originality."

B. **Incorrect**. If anything, the passage supports the opposite conclusion, in saying that "building according to formulas does not make good buildings."

C. **Incorrect**. The passage does not address the potential results of following unfamiliar forms in creating buildings.

D. **Correct**. The passage says that the similarities between Roman villas and earlier Greek temples show that great architects can be inspired by other architects. Thus, the passage implies that some Roman architects were great. Then the passage says that a great architect "creates fresh architectural compositions out of familiar forms." So it follows that some Roman architecture—the architecture created by the great Roman architects—exemplifies the creation of fresh architectural compositions out of familiar forms.

E. **Incorrect**. The architectural features of Greek temples are not discussed in the passage; neither is the source of Greek architectural inspiration discussed.

▪ *Difficulty Level: Easy*

▪ *Tips and Pitfalls: Read questions carefully. If a question asks which statement is supported by the passage, do not choose a response just because it seems on independent grounds to be plausible or likely—you must pick a response based on the information given in the passage.*

Question 3 *(page 27)*

General Description: This question asks you to find the assumption required by the argument. In other words, find the statement whose truth is required if the argument is to succeed in demonstrating its conclusion.

A. **Incorrect.** The existence of other lakes in the area is irrelevant to the argument.

B. **Incorrect.** If response (B) turned out to be true, that might provide a reason why humans were in the area of the lake, but this particular explanation need not be assumed in order for the argument to succeed in demonstrating its conclusion.

C. **Incorrect.** It does not matter for the argument whether or not there were such remains in the lava, and the argument does not state or imply that there were no humans in the region prior to two million years ago. This was by far the most popular incorrect response.

D. **Incorrect.** The remains could have gotten into the lake in any number of other ways; to give just one, perhaps the people in the area put their dead into the lake.

E. **Correct.** If the bones were not already in the sediments when the lake dried up, that means that they got into the sediments later; that is, less than one-and-a-half million years ago. But then their existence would not provide evidence that there were human ancestors in western Asia between two million and one-and-a-half million years ago; that is, the conclusion of the argument would not follow if (E) is false.

■ *Difficulty Level: Medium difficulty*

■ *Tips and Pitfalls: Another way to think about the question of whether an assumption is required by an argument is to think about what happens to the argument if the assumption turns out to be false. If the argument cannot possibly succeed when the assumption is false, then the assumption is required by the argument. Also, when asked for a necessary assumption, be careful not to pick an assumption that is stronger or broader than what is strictly necessary for the argument to succeed, even if making that assumption might strengthen the argument.*

Question 4 *(page 27)*

General Description: This question asks you to find the response that can be inferred from the given passage. A statement that may well be true, but that is irrelevant to the passage, cannot be the best answer. Even a response that presents information consistent with the passage need not be the best answer. Rather, the passage must provide grounds or support for inferring the response in order for that response to be the best answer.

A. **Incorrect.** This statement is contradicted by the first sentence in the passage, which states that there are some bad writers who cannot become better writers.

B. **Incorrect.** This statement is consistent with the passage. The passage allows the possibility that all great writers had to be taught to become better writers, though it says (in the last sentence) that teaching is not sufficient for becoming a great writer. But the passage also allows the possibility that some great writers did not have to be taught to become better writers. Since both the statement and its opposite are consistent with the passage, the statement in response (B) cannot be inferred from the passage.

C. **Correct.** This follows from the first sentence: Since some people are bad writers who cannot improve their writing, and since bad writers would have to improve their writing as a precondition for becoming great writers, it follows that there are some people who are bad writers and who can never become great writers.

D. **Incorrect.** Given the passage, there may well be some bad writers who can become great writers, but it might be instead that no bad writers can become great writers. Since both the statement and its opposite are consistent with the passage, the statement in response (D) cannot be inferred from the passage.

E. **Incorrect.** The passage makes no claims about how a great writer could become an even better writer, so this response cannot be inferred from the passage.

■ *Difficulty Level: Medium difficulty*

■ *Tips and Pitfalls: If a question asks what can be properly inferred from the passage, do not choose a response simply because it is consistent with the passage. The correct response will be one that follows logically from the statements in the passage; that is, the one that is consistent with the passage, but whose opposite is **not** consistent with the passage.*

Question 5 (*page 28*)

General Description: This question asks you to identify the conclusion of an argument. To answer this sort of question, you must be able to distinguish the conclusion from other parts of an argument (such as its premises), as well as from other parts of the passage that may not be part of the argument at all.

A. **Incorrect.** The question of the accuracy of the prime minister's remarks does not arise in the passage. To be sure, the issue of the accuracy of the newspaper's translation of those remarks is discussed, but that is a different issue—and that discussion is not the conclusion of the editor's argument.

B. **Incorrect.** The question of whether the remarks ought to have been reported arises at best obliquely in the passage, and the passage does not discuss at all what factors might be relevant or irrelevant to that question.

C. **Incorrect.** Though this claim is made by the newspaper editor (in the second sentence), it is presented as evidence in support of the conclusion (that is, as a premise), not as the conclusion itself.

D. **Correct.** The newspaper editor's conclusion is stated in the passage as "[t]hose consequences will not be our fault," after which the evidence that is meant to support that conclusion is presented. This is the best answer.

E. **Incorrect.** The passage takes no stand on whether Salino's predictions about consequences are accurate or not; the passage says only what will be the case *if* those consequences actually come to pass.

■ *Difficulty Level: Medium difficulty*

■ *Tips and Pitfalls: In identifying an argument's conclusion, be careful to pick neither a statement that makes up part of the argument's evidence or premises, nor a statement that seems plausible, given the passage, but is not the actual conclusion drawn by the argument in the passage.*

Question 6 (*page 28*)

General Description: This question asks you to find an assumption on which the editor's argument depends. In other words, find the statement whose truth is required if the argument is to succeed in demonstrating its conclusion.

A. **Correct.** The editor presents two premises in support of the conclusion that the newspaper cannot be blamed for the consequences of its reporting: First, that the quotation was an acceptable translation, and second, that "no newspaper can fairly be blamed for the consequences of its reporting when that reporting is accurate." For this second premise to have relevance to the first, it must be the case that reporting the acceptable translation was in fact reporting accurately; that is, response (A) must be assumed to be true.

B. **Incorrect.** The editor need not assume that newspapers should not consider the consequences of their coverage; the point of the argument is that the newspaper should not be blamed for such consequences, if the reporting was accurate.

C. **Incorrect.** The editor is not taking a stand on the question of whether any adverse consequences will actually occur, and so need not assume response (C). The point of the argument is just that if they do occur, the newspaper should not be blamed for them, if the newspaper's reporting was accurate.

D. **Incorrect.** This statement is irrelevant to the editor's argument.

E. **Incorrect.** The editor does presume that confirmation of a translation's accuracy by Qinkoan officials and scholars suffices to show that the translation is, in fact, accurate. But the editor does not (and need not) assume that this would be the only way to certify the accuracy of such a translation.

■ *Difficulty Level: Medium difficulty*

■ *Tips and Pitfalls: Another way to think about the question of whether an assumption is required by an argument is to think about what happens to the argument if the assumption turns out to be false. If the argument cannot possibly succeed when the assumption is false, then the assumption is required by the argument.*

Question 7 *(page 28)*

General Description: This question asks you to determine which response most strengthens the argument. In approaching such questions, you should identify the conclusion of the argument, and find the response that, if true, adds to the argument's support for its conclusion.

(A.) Correct. The argument says that automobile manufacturers addressed the trade-off between efficiency and safety by designing two kinds of cars, a more efficient but less safe car for local travel, and a less efficient but safer car for long-distance travel. Further, the argument says that "most automobile traffic is local," and then draws its conclusion that "a net savings in fuel use was achieved [with the two car designs] with no loss in safety." The more people actually use cars in the way that leads to greatest efficiency and safety, the stronger the argument is: That is, to the extent that people actually use the more efficient cars for local travel and the safer cars for long-distance travel, the argument is stronger. Response (A) strengthens the argument by showing that it is at least possible that most people do use their cars in that way, and is the best answer.

B. **Incorrect**. At best, the increased number of cars using high-speed highways is essentially irrelevant to the argument.

C. **Incorrect**. Without further information, it is not clear how the truth of this statement would bear on the argument. According to the passage, lighter cars are more fuel-efficient, but less safe. From response (C) alone, we cannot tell to what extent its truth would affect the net relationship between safety and fuel efficiency.

D. **Incorrect**. The relationship of commercial vehicles to the situation described in the passage does not arise in the argument; thus this response is, without further information, irrelevant to the argument.

E. **Incorrect**. This response is at best irrelevant to the argument; exactly when automobile manufacturers began designing fuel-efficient cars is not at issue.

■ *Difficulty Level: Relatively easy*

■ *Tips and Pitfalls: In answering a question asking for strengthening evidence, be careful not to read more into a response statement than is actually there. A statement that could strengthen the argument, if other (unstated) facts obtain, is not as good an answer as a statement that strengthens the argument on its own.*

Question 8 *(page 28)*

General Description: This question asks you to determine which response most weakens the argument. In approaching such questions, you should identify the conclusion of the argument, and find the response that, if true, undermines the argument's support for its conclusion.

A. **Incorrect**. If anything, this statement would tend to strengthen the argument, by eliminating a reason people might not actually use the lighter, more efficient cars.

B. **Incorrect**. This statement tends to strengthen the argument, by asserting that part of what the argument takes for granted (namely, that long-distance travel tends to take place on high-speed highways) is actually true.

C. **Incorrect**. The number of fuel-efficient cars being produced, and the distribution of such cars among the various automobile manufacturers, is irrelevant to the argument.

(D.) Correct. The argument is weakened to the extent that local travel takes place on high-speed highways. The argument says that "lighter, more efficient vehicles were less safe on high-speed highways." So if people use the more efficient but lighter, less-safe cars for local travel, and much local travel takes place on high-speed highways, the argument's conclusion that there is "no loss in safety" associated with the savings in fuel use is undermined.

E. **Incorrect**. The average passenger vehicle weight is irrelevant to the argument.

■ *Difficulty Level: Easy*

■ *Tips and Pitfalls: It may seem obvious to say that if the question asks for weakening evidence, one should not choose strengthening evidence, and vice versa, but this is an easy mistake to make when answering questions quickly. If a statement does not strengthen an argument, do not assume that it must therefore weaken the argument.*

Question 9 *(page 29)*

General Description: This question asks you to find the description of the method by which the argument proceeds.

A. **Incorrect**. The argument does offer several pieces of evidence, but they do not point to the conclusion independently of one another. That is, taking any one of the argument's pieces of evidence alone does not support the conclusion; it is only together that the evidence supports the conclusion.

B. **Correct**. The "phenomenon" is the nineteenth-century practice of recording poetry for noncommercial purposes. The "two subtypes" are (i) "[those made as] rare private souvenirs of the voices of famous poets" and (ii) "[those made] as publicity stunts, in which actors recorded poems that were familiar to the public." In the "particular case" of the recording in question, the argument eliminates the second subtype by pointing out that the poem on that recording "was never even published," that is, is not a poem that would likely have been familiar to the public. Since this response most completely and accurately describes the method of the argument in the passage, it is the best answer.

C. **Incorrect**. There are several statements in the passage that could be construed as "general principle[s]," but the argument does not attempt to demonstrate that any of them is violated in the particular case in question.

D. **Incorrect**. There are "two apparently mutually exclusive alternatives" presented— namely, that a certain recording of poetry made in the nineteenth century was made either as a souvenir of the voice of a famous poet, or else as a publicity stunt in which an actor recorded a well-known poem. But the argument does not attempt to show that these two alternatives are compatible with one another.

E. **Incorrect**. The argument can be construed as "explaining the historical context of an incident," though it may be debatable whether a recording counts as an "incident." But even if it does, this response is incorrect, because the argument does not attempt to demonstrate that two scenarios are equally likely. On the contrary, the argument purports to show that one scenario is more likely than the other.

■ **Difficulty Level:** *Difficult*

■ ***Tips and Pitfalls:*** *In answering questions about an argument's method, be careful to compare completely the methods of support described in the responses to the argument in the passage: If a response's method does not correspond exactly to that used in the argument, that response is not the best answer.*

Question 10 *(page 29)*

General Description: This question asks you to find the criticism to which the reasoning of the argument in the passage is most vulnerable.

Ⓐ **Correct**. The argument in the passage presents no real evidence for its conclusion. Saying that "it is better if everyone… provides the same amount of support" is practically equivalent to saying "[everyone] ought to contribute equally." So presenting the first as "evidence" for the second is simply to commit the error described in response (A).

B. **Incorrect**. The argument is not vulnerable to this criticism, because its claims are not tied to any "certain specified conditions."

C. **Incorrect**. There are no terms in the argument that could be characterized as "emotionally charged."

D. **Incorrect**. No group of people is being "judged wrong" in the argument; the argument is not vulnerable to this criticism.

E. **Incorrect**. It could be argued that this response is partly accurate, inasmuch as the argument presents the alternatives (i) all coffee drinkers contribute equally and (ii) coffee drinkers pay for their coffee by the cup. But the argument does not treat these two alternatives as if they exhaust the possibilities; note the reference to "some other manner."

■ *Difficulty Level: Relatively easy*

■ *Tips and Pitfalls: In a question that asks for a criticism of an argument's reasoning, for a response to be the best answer, it is necessary, but **not** sufficient, that it accurately describe some part of the argument. More than this, it must describe a feature of the argument in virtue of which the argument's reasoning is vulnerable to criticism.*

Question 11 *(page 29)*

General Description: This question asks you to find the response that would resolve the apparent discrepancy described in the passage. To answer this question, you must understand just what makes the evidence cited into an apparent discrepancy: What is the problem that the correct response will solve?

A. **Incorrect**. This information about the total market for clothing sales does not help resolve a discrepancy in the behavior of one particular clothing manufacturer.

B. **Incorrect**. Without further information, it is impossible to know how the employees' demands bear on the situation described in the passage. Even with further information, it is difficult to see how response (B) could bear on the second part of the discrepancy in the passage (closing the factory in response to reduced demand).

Ⓒ **Correct**. If the selling prices for Fabrico's products were 42 percent higher in 1987 than in 1986, but the total dollar amount of Fabrico's sales were only 17 percent higher in 1987 than in 1986, that suggests that Fabrico actually sold less clothing in 1987 than in 1986. Thus it is not surprising that Fabrico would close a factory in January 1988 because of reduced demand. Response (C) shows how both pieces of information in the passage could be true; that is, it resolves the discrepancy and is the best answer.

D. **Incorrect**. This statement could help explain the first part of the discrepancy (increased sales), but if anything, it makes the second part (closing the factory in response to reduced demand) even more mysterious.

E. **Incorrect**. The amount Fabrico spends on capital improvements has an impact on its overall profit, but overall profit is not at issue in the passage: The apparent discrepancy is that Fabrico has increased sales of its products and yet claims that demand for those products is reduced.

■ *Difficulty Level: Relatively easy*

■ *Tips and Pitfalls: In answering a question about resolving the discrepancy between two pieces of information, remember that the correct answer must explain both pieces of information. An answer that explains only one of the pieces of information is a tempting choice, but cannot be the correct answer to a question that asks you to resolve a discrepancy.*

Question 12 *(page 29)*

General Description: This question asks you to find the principle that would most help justify Saskia's position in arguing against Gerrit. To do so, it is important that you understand exactly what Saskia's position is, and how it is supported.

A. **Incorrect**. This principle would actually help establish Gerrit's position, not Saskia's. If the principle in response (A) were established, it would follow that the retailer was morally obligated to sell Gerrit the recording at the lower, mistaken price, since that was the price actually marked on the recording.

B. **Incorrect**. This principle would actually help establish Gerrit's position, not Saskia's. If the principle in response (B) were established, it would follow that Gerrit was morally entitled to profit from the retailer's mistake, that is, that he was morally entitled to purchase the recording at the lower, incorrect price.

C. **Incorrect**. Since the conversation in the passage does not address the question of updating prices in response to changes in manufacturers' suggested prices, this principle cannot help justify Saskia's position.

D. **Incorrect**. Since the retailer discussed in the passage did not intentionally encourage Gerrit to hold a certain expectation about the price of the recording (Gerrit says the price was "mistakenly" marked), the establishment of this principle cannot help justify Saskia's position.

 E. **Correct**. This principle presents a condition as necessary to create an obligation for a retailer to sell an item at a mismarked price: Only if the customer was "genuinely misled" about the price is such an obligation created. Since Gerrit was not genuinely misled about the price by the mismarking, the principle's necessary condition for such an obligation does not obtain in this case. That is, establishing the principle in response (E) would help justify Saskia's position that there is no such obligation in this case.

■ *Difficulty Level: Easy*

■ *Tips and Pitfalls: To justify one side's position, it is not sufficient that a principle undermine the opposing side's position; the correct response must provide positive support for the position in question.*

Question 13 *(page 30)*

General Description: This question asks you to identify an issue over which the treasure hunter and the archaeologist disagree. The task, then, is a matter of determining which of the choices is a claim supported by one speaker but rejected by the other.

A. **Incorrect.** Whether or not shipwrecks (or anything else, for that matter) count as archaeological artifacts does not arise in the passage.

B. **Correct.** The treasure hunter presents a rule applying to "a ship in peril" and claims that this rule applies also to the case of treasure hunters taking cargo from ancient shipwrecks. Thus the treasure hunter is saying that ancient shipwrecks count as "ships in peril" in the sense used in "centuries-old maritime law." The archaeologist, on the other hand, disagrees with this claim. By saying "these shipwrecks have stabilized over the centuries," the archaeologist shows disagreement with the claim that ancient shipwrecks are "ships in peril." By saying "[t]he only danger they are in is from greedy treasure hunters," the archaeologist suggests a different sense in which ancient shipwrecks may be said to be in peril. Thus the treasure hunter and the archaeologist disagree over "in what sense, if any, an ancient shipwreck can be said to be in peril."

C. **Incorrect.** The treasure hunter clearly believes that treasure hunters risk their lives in retrieving such artifacts, as shown by the reference in the last sentence to "cargo from ancient shipwrecks that they [i.e., treasure hunters] risk their lives to save." However, nothing the archaeologist says indicates disagreement with this claim. The archaeologist does make a claim about danger to the *shipwrecks*, but not about possible dangers to those who would retrieve their cargo. This was by far the most popular incorrect response.

D. **Incorrect.** The treasure hunter does bring maritime law into the discussion, but the archaeologist does not even address this issue in responding to the treasure hunter.

E. **Incorrect.** The treasure hunter brings into the discussion the general issue of the ownership of archaeological artifacts found on public property, but nothing the archaeologist says indicates any disagreement with the implication that antique shipwrecks can be said to be on public property.

■ **Difficulty Level:** *Difficult*

■ **Tips and Pitfalls:** *In a "point of disagreement" question, a choice that presents a claim that is supported or denied by one speaker, but about which the other speaker has made no commitment either way, cannot be correct. In other words, for a response to be the correct response, it is not sufficient that the speakers might disagree about it. Limit your analysis to what is actually said; avoid the temptation to speculate about what (else) either speaker might believe.*

Question 14 *(page 30)*

General Description: In looking for the response that most helps to explain the situation presented in the passage, first try to understand the situation. Then decide what it is about that situation that might need to be explained.

A. **Incorrect.** The containers for the two groups of flies are said to be "identical." So a claim comparing rates of oxygen consumption in containers of different sizes cannot help explain the difference in the flies' life spans.

B. **Correct.** The passage says that the flies in the colder environment (the ones that lived longer than six months) "consumed oxygen much more slowly" than the other flies. If consuming oxygen produces a toxic substance that accumulates until it eventually kills the fly, it stands to reason that the faster a fly consumes oxygen, the sooner it will die. Thus this claim, if true, helps explain why the colder flies lived longer: it is precisely because they consumed oxygen more slowly than the other flies.

C. **Incorrect.** The number of containers of flies of the two sorts is irrelevant to the situation described in the passage.

D. **Incorrect.** The passage says nothing about the presence of spiders in the containers with the flies. Furthermore, no information is given in the passage about the relation, if any, between a spider's consumption of oxygen and its ability to prey on flies.

E. **Incorrect.** The containers for both groups of flies are said to be "small," and in fact "identical." So a claim about flies in "small containers" cannot help explain a difference between the two groups of flies; the containers were all small.

■ *Difficulty Level: Easy*

■ *Tips and Pitfalls: In a question about explaining a situation, do not choose a response simply because it seems plausible. The correct response will contribute information that helps explain or resolve the situation described in the passage.*

Question 15 *(page 30)*

General Description: This question requires you to find the response that identifies a discrepancy in the proposal described in the passage for replacing a dangerous wild mosquito population with a harmless population.

A. **Incorrect.** The passage merely describes the three candidate genes; it makes no presuppositions about how easy or difficult the various genes would be to isolate and insert into the mosquitoes' cells.

B. **Correct.** The "goal of the proposal" is to replace the dangerous mosquito population with a harmless population. The first candidate gene would undermine this goal by threatening the survival of the new population: If the mosquitoes cannot find mates, then the survival of the new population is in jeopardy. The third candidate gene would also undermine this goal: if the mosquitoes' resistance to disease is "disabled," then the survival of the new population is at least threatened. This is the best answer.

C. **Incorrect.** While it is true that the proposal in the passage does not explicitly take into account positive roles that mosquitoes play in the environment, that is not a discrepancy in the proposal, as is called for in the question.

D. **Incorrect.** While it is true that none of the proposed alternatives would necessarily reduce the number of mosquitoes in any given area, that is not the goal of the proposal. The goal is to change the sort of mosquitoes in the wild, not to reduce their number. So this response does not identify a discrepancy in the proposal.

E. **Incorrect.** While it is true that no such evidence has been presented, that is not a discrepancy in the proposal, as is called for in the question.

■ *Difficulty Level: Medium difficulty*

■ *Tips and Pitfalls: For a response to be the best answer, it is necessary, but **not** sufficient, that it accurately describe some features of the proposal: It must also describe a discrepancy in the proposal.*

Question 16 *(page 31)*

General Description: This question requires you to determine which response is most supported by the information given. In answering this sort of question, look for the choice that has the firmest grounding in the claims made in the passage.

A. **Incorrect**. The passage gives no information about how the zebra mussels came to be in the Great Lakes, nor does it discuss the relationship, if any, between zebra mussels and species of clams native to those lakes.

B. **Incorrect**. The passage provides no basis for this speculation.

C. **Incorrect**. The passage does call the zebra mussels a "nuisance" in the intake pipes of nuclear power plants and water plants, but that does not mean that there is no mechanical way to remove the zebra mussels from the pipes. In other words, the existence of such a removal method would not necessarily keep the mussels from being a nuisance, depending on the nature of the method.

D. **Incorrect**. The passage provides no support for this claim. The mussels' removal of the algae is said to "significantly improve water quality" and "remov[e] some hazardous wastes" from the water, but there is no suggestion that removing the algae has any effect on the intake pipes' tendency to become clogged.

E. **Correct**. If the mussels remove hazardous waste from the water and do not transform that waste, the waste can be nowhere else but in the mussels. Thus there is reason to suppose that the mussels themselves become hazardous waste, though the passage does not show that this *must* be the case.

■ *Difficulty Level: Very difficult*

■ *Tips and Pitfalls: Pay careful attention to the level of support called for in the question. In this case the correct response must be supported, but need not be absolutely proven by the information in the passage.*

Question 17 *(page 31)*

General Description: To answer this question, you must first recognize the pattern or structure of the reasoning in the argument in the passage. Then choose the response whose argument is most like it in pattern or structure.

A. **Incorrect**. This argument, like that in the passage, presents one premise in which each of two possibilities is said to lead to a certain result. But here, unlike in the passage, the premise does not present the two possibilities as exhaustive, that is, as the only ways to lead to that result. Further, in response (A), the argument's second premise presents evidence that the result has not occurred in a particular case, and concludes that one of the possibilities must not have occurred either; thus it is unlike the argument in the passage in its pattern of reasoning.

B. **Incorrect**. This argument, unlike that in the passage, presents a premise in which a certain possibility is said to lead to one or the other of two results. Thus this argument is different in reasoning pattern from that in the passage.

C. **Correct**. This argument, like that in the passage, presents one premise in which each of two possibilities is said to lead to a certain result, and says that these two possibilities exhaust the ways of achieving that result. Then the argument concludes that in a particular case, one of the possibilities is actual, from evidence that the result occurred but that the other possibility did not. The argument in the passage proceeds in a similar pattern; thus this is the best answer.

D. **Incorrect**. This argument, like that in the passage, presents one premise in which each of two possibilities is said to lead to a certain result, and says that these two possibilities exhaust the ways of achieving that result. But the argument's second premise presents evidence that one of the possibilities did not occur, and concludes that the other possibility did not occur either. Thus this argument is different in its pattern of reasoning from the argument in the passage.

E. **Incorrect**. This argument, unlike that in the passage, presents a premise in which a certain condition is said to be necessary for either of two results to occur. Thus this argument is different in reasoning pattern from the argument in the passage.

■ *Difficulty Level: Medium difficulty*

■ *Tips and Pitfalls: In identifying an argument's pattern of reasoning, do not be concerned with the order in which the premises and conclusion of the argument happen to occur. The pattern of reasoning has to do with the functioning of those parts in the argument, not the order in which they happen to be presented.*

Question 18 *(page 32)*

General Description: This question asks you to find the response that would most strongly counter the city official's response to the citizen's argument about an increasing murder rate in their city and what the rate demonstrates about law enforcement's success at preventing violent crime.

A. **Incorrect**. The incidence of nonviolent crime has little, if any, bearing on the questions of whether the murder rate is increasing and whether the law enforcement system can prevent violent crime.

B. **Incorrect**. This response is actually irrelevant to the topic under discussion. The question in dispute is whether or not the overall murder rate has decreased, not in what fashion it decreased— if indeed it did decrease.

C. **Incorrect**. This response would support the city official's argument, if it turns out to be true. If a murder is more likely to be reported now than in the past, then if all other things were equal, the official murder rate would be going up. But the official murder rate, as described by the city official, has actually gone down, so actual murders in that case would have decreased even more than is shown by the decrease in the official murder rate.

D. **Incorrect**. This response does seem to address the point being made by the city official, which may account for its being the most popular among the incorrect answers. But in fact, the response does not help counter the city official's remarks. The city official's point is simply that an increase in raw numbers of murders does not show an increase in the murder rate, if the population is also increasing. The judgment of experts about the necessary number of law enforcement officials is beside the point.

E. **Correct**. The citizen takes an increase in the number of murders to demonstrate "the decreasing ability of our law enforcement system to prevent violent crime." The city official is arguing that an increase in raw numbers of murders does not show an increase in murder overall, if the population is also increasing, and suggesting that the number of murders per 100 people is a more meaningful figure. When considered in this way, according to the city official, "the number of murder *victims*… has actually fallen slightly." (emphasis added). Response (E), however, points out an alternative explanation for this fact. If response (E) is true, it could well be that more people are being attacked with deadly force, but people who in 1970 would have died (i.e., been murder victims) survived the attack last year, simply because the medical care they received was better. In that case, a decrease in the murder rate does not show a decrease in violent crime. Thus response (E) counters the city official's response, and is the best answer.

- **Difficulty Level:** *Very difficult*

- **Tips and Pitfalls:** *Pay careful attention to the precise point being made by a statement that is to be countered. Responses that are relevant in some way to the general topic under discussion, but that do not address the exact point to be countered, cannot be correct.*

Question 19 *(page 32)*

General Description: This question asks you to find the assumption on which the argument depends. In other words, find the statement whose truth is required if the argument is to succeed in demonstrating its conclusion.

A. **Incorrect.** Though this statement may well be true, the argument does not depend on assuming that any particular phenomenon is responsible for a change in the way obscenity is defined.

B. **Incorrect.** The argument need not make this assumption. It is consistent with the statements made in the argument that the number of things that are considered obscene has decreased with the passage of time, but the argument can still succeed in demonstrating its conclusion even if the number of things that are considered obscene has remained constant, or increased, over time.

C. **Incorrect.** If anything, the argument is presuming the opposite of response (C), or at least that public opinion is part of the determination of the artistic value of a work of art ("recognized masterpieces," "considered obscene").

D. **Correct.** The argument's only evidence for its conclusion is that some works of art are recognized masterpieces today, but were considered obscene when first created. If it were the case that all currently recognized masterpieces that were once considered obscene were still considered obscene (that is, if response [D] were false), then it would have to be the case that all of the works of art referred to by the argument's premise are still considered obscene. But then the argument has presented no examples of something being considered obscene at one time but not at another, which would be required for the argument to show that what is considered obscene or not obscene has changed over time. In short, if response (D) is false, the argument cannot succeed; thus the argument depends on assuming response (D).

E. **Incorrect.** The argument claims only that some currently recognized masterpieces were once considered obscene. The argument can still succeed if there are other currently recognized masterpieces that have never been considered obscene, that is, if response (E) is false.

■ *Difficulty Level: Medium difficulty*

■ *Tips and Pitfalls: Another way to think about the question of whether an argument depends on a particular assumption is to think about what happens to the argument if the assumption turns out to be false. If the argument cannot possibly succeed when the assumption is false, then the argument depends on the assumption. Also, be careful not to choose an option just because it might well be true, if the argument does not depend on its being true.*

Question 20 *(page 32)*

General Description: This question asks you to find the assumption on which the argument relies. In other words, find the statement whose truth is required if the argument is to succeed in demonstrating its conclusion.

A. **Incorrect.** This statement is irrelevant to the argument presented in the passage.

B. **Incorrect.** This statement, if true, might serve as part of an explanation for the phenomenon described in the passage, but it is logically irrelevant to the argument presented.

C. **Correct.** The argument presents evidence that the percentages of released criminals arrested while under one of the two kinds of supervision are the same, and uses this evidence to support a conclusion that the percentages of released criminals who commit crimes while under one of the two kinds of supervision are also the same. But if a person who commits a crime while under intensive supervision is much more likely to be arrested for it than is a person who commits a crime while under routine supervision (that is, if response [C] is false), then the evidence about arrests does not demonstrate the corresponding claim about crimes, as the argument takes it to do. In short, if response (C) is false, the argument cannot succeed; thus the argument relies on the assumption in response (C).

D. **Incorrect.** The truth of response (D) may well help the argument, since response (D) suggests that intensive supervision may actually be less effective than routine supervision in preventing further crime. But the argument can still succeed even if (D) is false, since the argument claims only that intensive supervision is no more effective than is routine supervision.

E. **Incorrect.** Since the argument consistently compares percentages of arrests (and of released criminals who commit additional crimes), the actual numbers of people in the two groups is irrelevant to the argument.

■ *Difficulty Level: Difficult*

■ *Tips and Pitfalls: Another way to think about the question of whether an assumption is relied upon by an argument is to think about what happens to the argument if the assumption turns out to be false. If the argument cannot possibly succeed when the assumption is false, then the argument relies on the assumption. Also, in general, pay careful attention to whether a statement is about actual numbers or about percentages.*

Question 21 *(page 33)*

General Description: This question asks you to find a reason the strength of the bicycle safety expert's argument cannot be evaluated. That is, find a response that describes information that would need to be known to decide whether or not the argument is a good one.

A. **Incorrect.** The statistics presented in the argument do not presuppose the truth of the argument's conclusion.

B. **Correct.** If it turns out, for example, that nearly all bicycling takes place on the left, then the bicycle safety expert's argument is quite weak, since most of the accidents do not involve bicycling on the left. But if instead it turns out that hardly any bicycling takes place on the left, then the argument is quite strong, since a significant number of the accidents do involve bicycling on the left. So without knowing the percentage of bicycling that took place on the left, it is impossible to know whether the bicycle safety expert's argument is strong or weak. This is the best answer.

C. **Incorrect.** It is true that no such statistics are presented in the bicycle safety expert's argument. But those statistics would be irrelevant to evaluating the strength of the argument, which focuses exclusively on collisions between bicycles and automobiles, not on what share of all bike accidents these represent.

D. **Incorrect.** It is true that the bicycle safety expert's argument focuses exclusively on the safety issues involved in bicycling on the left. But that does not make the strength of the argument impossible to evaluate.

E. **Incorrect.** It is true that the bicycle safety expert's argument does not make this distinction, and an explanation of the statistics cited in that argument may well need to make the distinction. But the argument is not about the reasons for the statistics it cites; rather it is about what the statistics show about the relative safety of bicycling on the left.

■ *Difficulty Level: Very difficult*

■ *Tips and Pitfalls: In answering a question like this, be careful not to choose a response simply because it is true of the argument in question. The correct response must also point out a gap in the argument, in virtue of which its strength cannot be evaluated.*

Question 22 *(page 33)*

General Description: This question asks you to find the response that, if true, would most help to resolve the discrepancy between the statements made by the two speakers in the passage.

A. **Incorrect**. The truth of this statement might help explain the skeptic's claim: perhaps such places are already so safe for bicyclists that adding another law does not appreciably improve bicycle safety. But response (A) does nothing to address the discrepancy between the skeptic's claim and the claim made by the bicycle safety expert.

B. **Incorrect**. This statement is irrelevant to the conflict between the statements made by the skeptic and the bicycle safety expert.

C. **Correct**. The truth of this statement would provide an explanation for the claims made by the skeptic and the bicycle safety expert. If a law prohibiting riding on the left is enacted but not enforced, then it can be true both that riding on the left is more likely to lead to collisions with automobiles (as claimed by the bicycle safety expert) and that enacting such a law does not reduce the number of such collisions, since there would be no incentive to refrain from riding on the left.

D. **Incorrect**. The numbers of adult and child bicycle riders is irrelevant to the discussion in the passage, at least without further information about the riding practices of adults and children.

E. **Incorrect**. This claim is consistent with the statistics cited by the bicycle safety expert, but does nothing to explain the skeptic's claim that prohibiting riding on the left does not significantly reduce the number of collisions.

■ *Difficulty Level: Difficult*

■ *Tips and Pitfalls: In answering a question about resolving the discrepancy between two pieces of information, remember that the correct answer must explain both pieces of information. An answer that explains only one of the pieces of information is sometimes a tempting choice, but cannot be the correct answer to a question that asks you to resolve a discrepancy.*

Question 23 *(page 33)*

General Description: This question asks you to find the response that most clearly illustrates an application of the principle described in the passage.

A. **Incorrect**. The behavior of the government described in this response has little bearing on the incentives affecting the choices of private individuals.

B. **Incorrect**. It is not at all obvious how, if at all, the choices of "voters in general" would be affected by the government's behavior in this case. Furthermore, without more information, it is impossible to say whether the government's behavior would affect the choices of the suspects whose rights are addressed by the bill.

C. **Incorrect**. The behavior of the government described in this response may affect the choices of the laid-off government workers, but it is not at all clear that it does so in a way that ensures they make "the best choice for the community," as is required by the principle in the passage.

D. **Incorrect**. In this case, the government's behavior may affect choices made by voters, but it is not at all clear that it does so in a way that ensures they make "the best choice for the community," as is required by the principle in the passage.

E. **Correct**. An increase in the electricity rate in the face of impending shortages is an incentive that helps ensure that the best choice for individuals is the best choice for the community. Presumably, if electricity is more expensive, people will choose to use less of it (to the extent possible), and making that choice will also help prevent shortages, which is in the best interest of the community.

■ *Difficulty Level: Very difficult*

■ *Tips and Pitfalls: Part of the difficulty in answering questions like this comes from the fact that you must fully understand the principle as well as each of the responses in order to choose the correct response. Read each response carefully and completely before choosing one.*

Question 24 (*page 34*)

General Description: This question asks you to identify the respect in which the reasoning in the passage's argument is flawed. That is, you must identify a logical weakness in the argument.

A. **Incorrect**. The argument does discuss "closely related aspects" of the discipline of economics (namely, properties of the discipline and properties of its practitioners), but the problem with the argument is just that it does *not* sufficiently treat these as distinct.

B. **Incorrect**. The argument does not attack the proponents of any claim.

C. **Incorrect**. The argument does not "insist on a change in terminology." The terminology in question is whether to describe economics as a science. The argument says only that "many professional economists" describe economics in this way—it is not clear that there is an established "terminology" at all. Further, the passage does not "insist" that economics not be described as a science, but rather argues for this view.

D. **Correct**. The first sentence reports the view of "many professional economists" about the nature of economics as a discipline: they describe it as a science. The argument goes on to present evidence about the nature of the work done by people who practice that discipline (i.e., "economists"). But a discipline and its practitioners are on the face of it quite different: in particular, the argument gives no reason to think that if a discipline is descriptive, its practitioners cannot offer prescriptive recommendations. So the argument makes the mistake described in response (D).

E. **Incorrect**. The argument does not overlook this necessity; the issue of division of labor within society does not arise in the passage.

■ *Difficulty Level:* Difficult

■ *Tips and Pitfalls:* In answering a question about a reasoning flaw, keep in mind that for a response to be the best answer, it is necessary, but **not** sufficient, that it accurately describe some part of the argument: it must describe a feature of the argument in virtue of which the argument's reasoning is flawed.

Question 25 (*page 34*)

General Description: This question asks you to find the response that contains a pattern of flawed reasoning most similar to that contained in the passage's argument. To do this, you must understand the flawed pattern in the passage's argument. Then choose the response that exhibits the most similar flawed pattern.

A. **Incorrect**. This argument is not flawed. Its premises, if true, provide good evidence for drawing its conclusion.

B. **Incorrect**. This argument is flawed in generalizing from a specific case that may not be representative. But that is not the flawed pattern in the passage's argument.

C. **Incorrect**. This argument is not flawed. Its premises, if true, provide good evidence for drawing its conclusion.

D. **Correct**. Just because most As are Bs, that does not mean a particular B is likely to be an A. There may be many more Bs than As. This is the flaw in the passage, and in response (D).

E. **Incorrect**. This argument is not flawed. Its premises, if true, provide good evidence for drawing its conclusion.

■ *Difficulty Level:* Very difficult

■ *Tips and Pitfalls:* When asked to find a similar reasoning error, it is often helpful to look at the passage and responses from a structural point of view; the topics of the passage and responses are irrelevant to the question of the pattern of flawed reasoning. Also, if you can securely identify a response as presenting an unflawed argument (in this case, [A], [C], and [E]), then you can eliminate that response from contention: It cannot contain a similar pattern of flawed reasoning if it does not contain a pattern of flawed reasoning at all.

Analytical Reasoning: Questions 1-24

Passage *(page 35):* The passage essentially requires you to schedule seven jobs over five days (Monday through Friday). For a schedule to be acceptable it must not violate any information contained in the passage. There are several different acceptable schedules one can create, but all of them must have X on Wednesday by itself, and T on Friday. Although some acceptable schedules will have a second job assigned to Friday, others will not. Remember also that every acceptable schedule will have U assigned to a day by itself regardless of what day U is assigned to, and that N and S must be assigned to the same day as each other.

Question 1 *(page 35)*

Strategy: Take each response and go through the conditions one by one, eliminating any response that violates one or more of the conditions.

A.   **Incorrect.** The fourth condition states that U must take an entire day. Since it is stipulated that no two jobs are done concurrently, O and U cannot be done on the same day.

B.   **Incorrect.** The second condition requires that T be done on Friday. Not only is T not done on Friday—it is not done at all, which also violates the requirement that all seven of the jobs must be done.

C.   **Incorrect.** The third condition requires that S be done earlier than the day on which P is done. Thus, P cannot be done on Monday.

D.   **Incorrect.** The first condition stipulates that N and S are done on the same day.

E.   **Correct.** This is the only response that meets all of the conditions given in the passage.

■ *Difficulty Level: Easy*

Question 2 *(page 35)*

Strategy: For each response, determine whether each of the jobs listed can be done on Tuesday. If even one of the jobs listed can be done on Tuesday, eliminate the response from consideration. Once you've determined that a particular job can be done on Tuesday, immediately eliminate any other response that includes that job.

A.   **Incorrect.** P can be done on Tuesday. Assign N and S to Monday. Since X is done on Wednesday and T on Friday, U would have to be done on Thursday. O could be done either on Friday or on Tuesday.

B.   **Correct.** The second condition requires that X be done on Wednesday and T on Friday. So neither T nor X can be done on Tuesday. To see that this list is complete see the explanations for the other responses.

C.   **Incorrect.** N can be done on Tuesday with S as long as P is done some day later. One possibility is to have P done on Friday with T, U on Thursday, and O on Monday.

D.   **Incorrect.** N can be done on Tuesday with S as long as P is done some day later. One possibility is to have P done on Friday with T, U on Thursday, and O on Monday.

E.   **Incorrect.** U can be done on Tuesday, with N and S being done on Monday, X on Wednesday, P and O on Thursday, and T on Friday.

■ *Difficulty Level: Relatively easy*

Question 3 *(page 35)*

Strategy: To eliminate a response, try to produce an acceptable schedule where O is done on Thursday and N on some day other than those listed in the response. With this and other questions that ask you what must or could be true given a particular possibility, it is worth trying to first rule out responses using the original conditions alone, before using the specific situation given in the question.

As an alternative strategy, map out all the possible setups in which O is done on Thursday and then choose the response that describes the resulting possibilities for N.

A. **Incorrect.** N can be done on Tuesday (with S): Assign U to Monday, X to Wednesday, O and P to Thursday, and T to Friday.

B. **Incorrect.** N can be done on Tuesday (with S): Assign U to Monday, X to Wednesday, O and P to Thursday, and T to Friday.

C. **Correct.** N cannot be done later in the week than Tuesday; it can't be done on Wednesday, since X must be done alone then. Since no more than two jobs can be done in one day, N cannot be done on Thursday (with O) or Friday (with T), because S must be done with N. To see that N could be done on Monday, see the explanation for (D), and to see that it could be done on Tuesday, see the explanation for (A).

D. **Incorrect.** N can be done on Monday (with S): Assign U to Tuesday, X to Wednesday, P and O to Thursday, and T to Friday.

E. **Incorrect.** N can be done on Monday (with S): Assign U to Tuesday, X to Wednesday, P and O to Thursday, and T to Friday.

■ *Difficulty Level: Easy*

Question 4 *(page 35)*

Strategy: Eliminate responses by trying to construct an acceptable schedule wherein two jobs are done on Thursday and two others on Friday; then determine what range of possibilities conforms with this condition. Note that seven jobs have to be done in five days, with a maximum of two jobs per day. So there are exactly two days that have two jobs each done on them.

A. **Incorrect.** N must be done on Thursday with S, which, together with the third condition, means P must be the other job done on Friday. U can be done on either Monday or Tuesday, O being done on the day U is not.

B. **Incorrect.** O can be done on Monday so long as U is done on Tuesday, X on Wednesday, N and S on Thursday, and T and P on Friday.

C. **Correct.** Given the first condition, N and S must be one of the pairs of jobs done on one day. They can't be done on Friday because T is done on Friday, so they have to be done on Thursday. The third condition thus requires that P be done on Friday.

D. **Incorrect.** O can be done by itself on Monday so long as U is done on Tuesday, X on Wednesday, N and S on Thursday, and T and P on Friday.

E. **Incorrect.** O can be done by itself on Monday so long as U is done on Tuesday, X on Wednesday, N and S on Thursday, and T and P on Friday.

■ *Difficulty Level: Relatively easy*

Question 5 *(page 35)*

Strategy: Eliminate responses by producing acceptable schedules that contradict the assignments in the responses. For (A) through (C) this means assigning the job designated in the response to some day other than those mentioned in the response. For (D) and (E) it suffices to create an acceptable schedule where the first job mentioned in the response is done by itself. Note that since P is not done on Friday, it must be done either on Tuesday or Thursday, given the third condition and the fact that X is the only job done on Wednesday.

A.   **Incorrect.** N can be done on Tuesday with S. With this assignment, U will have to be done on Monday, X on Wednesday, and P on Thursday. O may be done on Thursday with P or on Friday with T.

B.   **Incorrect.** O can be done on Friday with T. With this assignment, N and S can be done on Monday, U on Tuesday, X on Wednesday, and P on Thursday.

C.   **Incorrect.** S can be done on Tuesday with N. With this assignment, U will have to be done on Monday, X on Wednesday, and P on Thursday. O may be done on Thursday with P or on Friday with T.

D.   **Incorrect.** P can be done alone on Thursday. With this assignment, N and S can be done on Monday, U on Tuesday, X on Wednesday, and O on Friday with T. This was the most difficult response to eliminate.

E.   **Correct.** O cannot be done on the same day as X, U, N, or S: X and U are full-day jobs, while N and S together take up a full day. P is done either on Tuesday or on Thursday (see strategy). Suppose first that P is done on Tuesday, then N and S must be done on Monday, and U on Thursday. Thus, O must be done either on Tuesday with P, or on Friday with T. On the other hand, if P is done on Thursday, then N and S must be done on either Monday or Tuesday, with U being done on the day on which N and S are not. This means O must be done on Thursday with P, or on Friday with T. In either event, O must be done either with P or with T.

■ *Difficulty Level: Medium difficulty*

Question 6 *(page 35)*

Strategy: To eliminate a response, try to create a schedule that has the job mentioned in the response done on a day other than that designated in the response. Note that by assigning O to Monday, Tuesday and Thursday are the only full days left on which to place U (since it is an all-day job) or N and S (since together they take a whole day).

A.   **Incorrect.** N and S can be done on Thursday. This requires that U be done on Tuesday, and P with T on Friday. This was the most popular incorrect selection.

B.   **Incorrect.** N and S can be done on Thursday and P with T on Friday. This requires that U be done on Tuesday.

C.   **Correct.** As the strategy points out, Tuesday and Thursday must be assigned, in either order, U or the pair of N and S or U. This leaves Monday and Friday as possible days for P. Since O is assigned to Monday, P must be done on Friday.

D.   **Incorrect.** S can be done on Tuesday with N. This requires that U be done on Thursday, and P with T on Friday.

E.   **Incorrect.** U requires an entire day, so it cannot be done with T, which must be done on Friday.

■ *Difficulty Level: Easy*

Passage *(page 36)*: The passage requires you to split up six of the seven climbers into three teams of two without violating any of the information in the passage. From the main body of the passage you know that the seventh person will be the organizer and will not be on any of the teams you create. You also know that no one can be on more than one team. While the first condition or rule is straightforward, the conditional nature of the remaining three conditions should be carefully noted. The second and third conditions merely provide for who else must be on a team *if* a particular person is known to be on that team. The final condition makes K the organizer if H is on a team. These conditions by themselves do not tell us who is actually on any team; so, for example, the second condition does not imply that K has to be on any of the teams. There are several immediate inferences you should make and take advantage of: If H is a member of any team, K cannot be a member of any team (third condition); if K is not the organizer, then K and M are going to form one of the teams; and finally, either H or K is the organizer.

Question 7 *(page 36)*

Strategy: As with most questions that present you with full solutions to evaluate, you can take each response and make sure the response meets each of the conditions and all of the information in the passage, or take each condition and apply it to each of the responses. Any response that violates one or more of the conditions or any of the information in the passage may be eliminated. Remember, for each of conditions two through four, if the first part of the condition does not apply to a particular response, then that response does not violate the condition.

A.   **Incorrect.** This violates the first condition.

B.   **Incorrect.** Note that H is on a team (Team 1), and so the fourth condition applies. This means K is the organizer and therefore cannot be on any team. However, this response has K on Team 3.

C.   **Correct.** This is the only response that meets all of the conditions given in the passage.

D.   **Incorrect.** G is on a team (Team 1), and so—according to the third condition—must be on the same team as either H or I, and not P as given in the response.

E.   **Incorrect.** This response violates the last condition in the same way response (B) does. It also violates the second condition.

■ *Difficulty Level: Easy*

Question 8 *(page 36)*

Strategy: This question requires you to look for the one response that violates one or another of the options. Thus, for each of the responses, see if you can form another two teams out of the remaining climbers without violating any of the conditions. If you can't, that response is the correct answer.

A.   **Correct.** If H and I are on a team: together, they can't be on a team with G, because the second condition requires G to be on a team with either H or I. So, G cannot be on any team, which means G has to be the organizer. But, according to the last condition, if H is on a team, then K must be the organizer. Since there can be only one organizer, we have to violate either the second or third condition if we are to have H and I on the same team as each other.

B.   **Incorrect.** H and M can be on a team together. G and I would have to make up one of the remaining teams, and L and P the other.

C.   **Incorrect.** I and M can be on a team together. G and H would have to make up one of the remaining teams, and L and P the other.

D.   **Incorrect.** I and P can be on a team together. G and H would have to make up one of the remaining teams, and L and M the other.

E.   **Incorrect.** There are several possibilities in which L and P form one of the teams. For example, the other two teams could be H and M, and G and I.

■ *Difficulty Level: Relatively easy*

Question 9 *(page 36)*

Strategy: This question essentially requires you to determine which of the people in the responses could be left out in forming the teams. One possible approach is to focus first on those people that the conditions suggest might not be on any team, i.e., K, G, and H. Since K is not among the possible responses, start with response (A) and try to form the three teams without G. If you can, then try to do the same for (B). Remember, if a particular person is the organizer, everyone else must be on a team.

A. **Incorrect.** If G is not on any team, K will have to be, but so will H. However, according to the last rule, if H is on a team, K must be the organizer and hence not on any team. So, G cannot be the organizer.

B. **Correct.** Either H or K must be the organizer. Since K is not among the responses, (B) must be correct.

C. **Incorrect.** If I is not on any team, then G has to be, and so must form a team with H. But if H is on a team then K cannot be. Since there can only be one organizer, I cannot be that organizer.

D. **Incorrect.** If L is not on any team, then K has to be on a team, as does H. However, according to the rules, if K is on a team, then H can't be and vice versa.

E. **Incorrect.** If P is not on a team, then K has to be on a team, as does H. However, according to the rules, if K is on a team, then H can't be and vice versa.

■ *Difficulty Level: Medium difficulty*

Question 10 *(page 36)*

Strategy: The question asks what you can determine about a team in which H is a member if G and I form one team. You need to note first that if G and I form a team, then the membership of only two teams remains undetermined. One approach is then to survey the conditions to find out what else can be discovered about the team in which H is a member.

A. **Incorrect.** By the last condition, K is the organizer. L can be on either the team with H or on the remaining undetermined team.

B. **Incorrect.** By the last condition, K is the organizer. P can be on either the team with H or on the remaining undetermined team.

C. **Incorrect.** L and M can both be on the remaining undetermined team, and P can be on the team with H.

D. **Incorrect.** L and P can both be on the remaining undetermined team, and M can be on the team with H.

E. **Correct.** Since, by the first condition, M and P cannot be on the same team, exactly one of either M or P is on the team with H, and exactly one of either M or P is on the remaining undetermined team.

■ *Difficulty Level: Relatively easy*

Question 11 *(page 36)*

Strategy: The question asks you what must be true if L and M are on different teams. One approach is to first determine what is known about the team structures under this assumption, and see which response captures some or all of what you have determined. Since H is either on a team or is the organizer, we know from the fourth condition that either H or K must be the organizer. Hence, G must be on a team, and, from the third condition, G must be on a team with either H or I. Hence, P cannot be on the same team as G. Also, given the first condition, P cannot be on the same team as M. Hence P must be on the same team as L.

A. **Incorrect.** H or K can be the organizer.

B. **Incorrect.** H or K can be the organizer.

C. **Incorrect.** If H is the organizer, I must be on the same team as G.

D. **Incorrect.** If H is the organizer, I must be on the same team as G.

E. **Correct.** As in the Strategy, since either H or I is on the same team as G, P must be on the team with L or the team with M. But by the first condition, P cannot be on the same team as M.

■ *Difficulty Level: Difficult*

Question 12 *(page 36)*

Strategy: This question asks you to identify the response that meets both of two criteria: None of the possible organizers must appear in the response, and no team can be formed from any two of the three persons in the response. Any response that has at least one pair that can form a team or a possible organizer can be ruled out immediately. Since we know either H or K must be the organizer, any response with either may be eliminated.

A. **Incorrect.** While according to the third condition G cannot be on a team with either L or M, L and M themselves could form a team. So this response does not meet the requirement that no two can be on the same team as each other.

B. **Correct.** G cannot be on a team with either M or P (condition 3), and M and P cannot form a team (condition 1). Finally, G, M, and P must all be on a team, since neither G, M, nor P can be an organizer (condition 4). This response meets both requirements and is therefore correct.

C. **Incorrect.** None of the pairings of H, I, and L are possible. However, following condition 4, either H or K must be the organizer. So this option is ruled out by the presence of H, who can be an organizer and thus does not have to be on a team. This response meets only one of the two criteria.

D. **Incorrect.** While I, L, and P must all be on a team, all pairings of I, L, and P can form teams. Like (A), this response does not meet the requirement that no two can be on the same team as each other.

E. **Incorrect.** While M and P cannot form a team, given the first condition, L and M and L and P can form teams. Again, this response does not meet the requirement that no two can be on the same team as each other.

■ *Difficulty Level: Medium difficulty*

Question 13 *(page 36)*

Strategy: You are asked to determine all the possible teams that M could form. The first condition allows us to infer that at least P cannot form a team with M. The second condition lets us know that at least K could form a team with M. The third condition requires that H or I be on the same team as G if G was on a team. So G cannot form a team with M. These considerations imply that at least one person can form a team with M, but that there must be less than five (allowing you to eliminate response [E]). You should now determine how many of the remaining three people (H, I, and L) could form a team with M.

A. **Incorrect.** M can form a team with H. The other teams could be G and I, and L and P. We know from the Strategy that K can form a team with M, thus at least two different people can form a team with M.

B. **Incorrect.** M can form a team with I. G and H can form one of the other teams, while L and P can form the other. From this consideration, the explanation for (A), and the Strategy, we know that at least three different people can form a team with M.

C. **Incorrect.** M can form a team with L. G and H can form one of the other teams, with I and P forming the other. From this consideration, the explanations for (A) and (B), and the Strategy, we know that at least four different people can form a team with M.

D. **Correct.** The explanations for (A) through (C) show that at least four different people can form a team with M. The Strategy shows that there can't be five different people who can form a team with M. Thus, exactly four different people can be the person who forms a team with M.

E. **Incorrect.** See the Strategy for this question.

■ *Difficulty Level: Difficult*

Passage *(page 37)*: The passage requires you to construct the five trips a train makes. There are five different stations at which the train can stop, but for each individual trip the train stops at exactly three of those stations. Over the course of the five trips the train has to have stopped at each of the five stations a total of three times. However, it cannot stop at any one of the stations on each of three consecutive trips. Furthermore, in the course of trip 1 and trip 2 the train must have stopped at each of the stations at least once. The same is true of trip 2 and trip 3, of trip 3 and trip 4, and of trip 4 and trip 5.

Question 14 *(page 37)*

Strategy: Here you are asked to determine which partial list of the trips is accurate. However, note that it is possible for a list of two trips not to violate any of the conditions by itself, and yet not be part of any acceptable list of the five trips. In other words, in solving this problem you should be sure the correct answer is part of an acceptable list of the five trips. Of course, if a response violates either (or both) of the conditions it is incorrect.

A. **Incorrect.** Since the train does not stop at T on either trip, this response violates the second condition.

B. **Incorrect.** Since the train does not stop at S on either trip, this response violates the second condition.

C. **Incorrect.** Since the train does not stop at T on either trip, this response violates the second condition.

D. **Correct.** Since the train stops at each of the stations at least once during the first two trips, this response meets the second condition. But in order to determine if this response is correct, one must make sure that it does not violate the first condition or any other requirements given in the passage. In order to do that, one should try to construct the remaining three trips. To construct each trip subsequent to the second, first determine which station has been stopped at on both trip 1 and trip 2. Here, that is S. According to the first condition, the train cannot stop at a particular station on three consecutive trips. Thus S cannot be among the train's stops on trip 3. Furthermore, since the second condition requires that the train stop at each of P, Q, R, S, and T at least once in any two consecutive trips, Q and T must be among the train's stops on trip 3 (since they were not among the train's stops on trip 2). There are two sets of stations that satisfy these requirements: P, Q, T and Q, R, T. It actually does not matter which one you choose (of course, what you do in fact choose will make a difference for the subsequent trips). Let us choose Q, R, T. We can apply similar reasoning to construct the remaining two trips. Since neither P nor S is among the train's stops on trip 3, they must be among the train's stops on trip 4. Since the train stopped at R on both trip 2 and trip 3, the train cannot stop at R on trip 4. Again, this leaves us with two possibilities: P, S, T and Q, P, S. Selecting P, S, T as stops on trip 4 permits us to select Q, P, R as the fifth and final stops on the trip.

E. **Incorrect.** Since the train does not stop at Q on either trip, it violates the second condition.

■ *Difficulty Level: Relatively easy*

Question 15 *(page 37)*

Strategy: You are given the first and third trips, and are then asked to determine the second trip. First use the second condition to determine from the first trip the stations at which the train must stop. Then apply the first condition to trips 1 and 3 to determine the stations at which the train cannot stop.

A. **Incorrect.** If the train stops at R on the second trip, it will have stopped at R on three consecutive trips by the end of trip 3. This violates the first condition.

B. **Correct.** From the second condition we know that the train must stop at P and T, since it did not do so on trip 1. From condition 2, we know that the train cannot stop at either R or S (since if it did it would violate the first condition). Thus, Q must be the remaining station.

C. **Incorrect.** If the train stops at S, it will have stopped at S on three consecutive trips by the end of trip 3. This violates the first condition.

D. **Incorrect.** If the train stops at R on the second trip, it will have stopped at R on three consecutive trips by the end of trip 3. This violates the first condition.

E. **Incorrect.** If the train stops at S, it will have stopped at S on three consecutive trips by the end of trip 3. This violates the first condition.

■ *Difficulty Level: Relatively easy*

Question 16 *(page 37)*

Strategy: There are two approaches to answering this question. The first is quite easy, but rather time-consuming: Create a full list of the five trips for each of the responses to see if P and Q can be stops on the trips listed in each response. If you *can* create a full list, then you may eliminate the response. The other approach to this question is to focus directly on the last condition and the fact that the train stops at only three stations per trip.

A. **Incorrect.** The following list of five trips shows that the train can stop at both P and Q on both the first and third trips:
Trip 1: P, Q, R; Trip 2: R, S, T; Trip 3: P, Q, S; Trip 4: Q, R, T; Trip 5: P, S, T.

B. **Incorrect.** The following list of five trips shows that the train can stop at both P and Q on both the first and fourth trips:
Trip 1: P, Q, R; Trip 2: P, S, T; Trip 3: Q, R, S; Trip 4: P, Q, T; Trip 5: R, S, T.

C. **Incorrect.** The following list of five trips shows that the train can stop at both P and Q on both the second and fourth trips:
Trip 1: Q, R, S; Trip 2: P, Q, T; Trip 3: R, S, T; Trip 4: P, Q, R; Trip 5: P, S, T.

D. **Incorrect.** The following list of five trips shows that the train can stop at both P and Q on both the second and fifth trips:
Trip 1: R, S, T; Trip 2: P, Q, R; Trip 3: Q, S, T; Trip 4: P, R, S; Trip 5: P, Q, T.

E. **Correct.** A general implication of the last condition is that the train cannot stop at any more than one particular station twice in the course of two consecutive trips. The last condition requires the train to stop at every station at least once in any two consecutive trips. Since there are five stations and since the train stops at only three stations per trip, stopping at both P and Q on each of two consecutive trips allows the train to stop at only two of the three other stations during those two trips. Thus, the train cannot stop at two stations twice in the course of two consecutive trips without violating the last condition. (E) violates this condition by having the train stop at both P and Q twice in the course of two consecutive trips.

■ *Difficulty Level: Very difficult*

Question 17 *(page 37)*

Strategy: You are asked to determine which one of the responses could be true if the train stops at the given stations on trips 1 and 4. For each response, suppose the response is true, and that the train stops at Q, R, and T on the first trip and at Q, R, and S on the fourth trip. If that does not lead to a violation of some condition or to some other contradiction, you have found the correct response.

(A.) **Correct.** The following list of five trips satisfies every condition, including those in the question: Trip 1: Q, R, T; Trip 2: P, Q, S; Trip 3: P, R, T; Trip 4: Q, R, S; Trip 5: P, S, T.

B. **Incorrect.** If the train stops at R on trip 5, that would be the third and final time the train stops at R. The other two times are given as the first trip and the fourth trip. But that would mean that the train does not stop at R on either trip 2 or trip 3, in violation of the second condition.

C. **Incorrect.** If the train stops at T on trip 2, it could not stop at T on trip 3 (otherwise it would violate the first condition, given that it stops at T on trip 1). Since it is given that the train does not stop at T on the fourth trip, it has to stop at T on the fifth trip in order to have stopped there exactly three times. But that would mean the train does not stop at T on either trip 3 or trip 4, in violation of the second condition.

D. **Incorrect.** If the train does not stop at P on trip 2, there will be two consecutive trips (trip 1 and trip 2) on which the train did not stop at P. This violates the second condition.

E. **Incorrect.** If the train does not stop at T on the fifth trip, then since (according to the question) it does not stop at T on the fourth trip either, it would have to stop at T on the first three trips in violation of the first condition.

■ *Difficulty Level: Very difficult*

Question 18 *(page 37)*

Strategy: This question begins by giving you a partial schedule of the train's stops that violates one of the conditions. It then asks you to select the response that corrects the schedule. The resulting correction must itself violate none of the conditions. The first thing to do is identify how the given partial schedule is mistaken. It is unacceptable in two respects: It violates the first condition (by having the train stop at S on three consecutive trips) and it violates the second condition (by failing to have the train stop at T at least once on one of the first two trips). Thus, the correct response will replace one of the first two stops at S with a stop at T.

A. **Incorrect.** If the train stops at P instead of at Q on the first stop, it still stops at S during three consecutive trips, and it still fails to stop at T at least once during the first two trips.

B. **Incorrect.** While stopping at R instead of S on the second trip does mean that the train does not stop at S on three consecutive trips, it now means that it stops at R on three consecutive trips. Furthermore, the train still does not stop at T at least once during the first two trips.

(C.) **Correct.** By stopping at T instead of S on the second trip, the train now no longer stops at S on three consecutive trips, and it now stops at T at least once in the course of the first two trips. To be thorough, we should show that five acceptable trips can be constructed with this substitution. The following list does this: Trip 1: Q, R, S; Trip 2: P, Q, T (note that this is the substitution given by the response); Trip 3: R, S, T; Trip 4: P, Q, S; Trip 5: P, R, T.

D. **Incorrect.** Not only does the train still stop at S on three consecutive trips with this substitution, it still fails to stop at T at least once during the first two trips. Furthermore, it now stops at P on three consecutive trips.

E. **Incorrect.** Although this substitution corrects the violation of the first condition, it does not correct the violation of the second condition: The train still does not stop at T at least once during the first two trips.

■ *Difficulty Level: Medium difficulty*

Passage *(page 38)*: This passage requires you to determine both the locations of six speakers' lectures and the order in which the speakers give their lectures. The lectures can be given in one of two locations: the studio and the library. The lectures are scheduled in three one-hour time slots at each location. Problems such as these are easily diagrammed. One may make a table with two rows (one for each location) and three columns (one for each time slot). The conditions governing the schedule are fairly straightforward, but care should be taken in recognizing what they allow. For instance, the second condition merely prevents Feinberg from lecturing earlier than Guzman; it does not prevent Feinberg from lecturing at the same time as Guzman. Likewise, the third condition merely prevents Jansen and Mackey from lecturing at the same time as Feinberg; it does not determine whether Jansen, for example, lectures before or after Feinberg. There is an immediate inference one should note: the fourth condition implies that Harrison cannot lecture at 10 A.M., and that Feinberg cannot lecture at 8 A.M.

Question 19 *(page 38)*

Strategy: You are asked which one of the responses must be true. One approach to solving questions such as this one is to try to falsify each response. That which you cannot falsify must be true, and therefore the correct response. Each of the responses states that one of exactly two people must lecture at a particular time in a particular place. To falsify such a statement one needs to see if it is possible for neither of the specified people to lecture at the time and place—that is, see if it is possible for both of the mentioned speakers to lecture at some other time and/or place.

 Correct. Both Jansen and Mackey must lecture in the studio. If neither lectures at 8 A.M. (i.e., if response [A] is false), they must lecture at 9 A.M. and 10 A.M. (for this question, it doesn't matter which of Jansen and Mackey lectures at 9 A.M.). The third condition requires that Feinberg lecture at some time other than Jansen and at some time other than Mackey. Thus, Feinberg would have to lecture at 8 A.M. But this makes it impossible to satisfy the fourth condition (requiring Jansen to lecture before Feinberg), since 8 A.M. is the earliest anyone can lecture. Therefore, either Jansen or Mackey must lecture at 8 A.M.

B. **Incorrect.** The following table shows that neither Harrison nor Mackey need lecture in the studio at 9 A.M.:

	8 A.M.	9 A.M.	10 A.M.
Library	Harrison	Guzman	Kim
Studio	Jansen	Feinberg	Mackey

You should be able to verify that this schedule meets all the conditions.

C. **Incorrect.** The following table shows that neither Guzman nor Harrison need lecture in the library at 8 A.M.:

	8 A.M.	9 A.M.	10 A.M.
Library	Kim	Harrison	Guzman
Studio	Mackey	Jansen	Feinberg

You should be able to verify that this schedule meets all the conditions.

D. **Incorrect.** The following table shows that neither Feinberg nor Guzman need lecture in the library at 9 A.M.:

	8 A.M.	9 A.M.	10 A.M.
Library	Kim	Harrison	Guzman
Studio	Mackey	Jansen	Feinberg

You should be able to verify that this schedule meets all the conditions.

E. **Incorrect.** The following table shows that neither Feinberg nor Guzman need lecture in the library at 10 A.M.:

	8 A.M.	9 A.M.	10 A.M.
Library	Harrison	Guzman	Kim
Studio	Jansen	Feinberg	Mackey

You should be able to verify that this schedule meets all the conditions.

■ *Difficulty Level: Difficult*

Question 20 *(page 38)*

Strategy: For each response, try to construct a schedule that has Kim and Mackey lecturing at 9 A.M. and that also makes the response true. Note that the fifth condition requires Mackey to lecture in the studio; thus for this question, Kim will have to lecture in the library at 9 A.M.

A. **Incorrect.** Suppose Guzman lectures at 8 A.M. Since Feinberg cannot lecture at 8 A.M. (implication of the fourth condition), and since all of the 9 A.M. slots are filled up, Feinberg would have to lecture at 10 A.M. Since Harrison has to lecture before Feinberg, Harrison has to lecture at 8 A.M. for the same reason (i.e., all of the 9 A.M. slots are gone). So now all of the 8 A.M. slots are filled up, forcing Jansen to lecture at 10 A.M.—the same time as Feinberg. This would violate the third condition.

B. **Incorrect.** This response violates the implication of the fourth condition.

C. **Incorrect.** Since Feinberg cannot lecture at 8 A.M. and since both 9 A.M. slots are filled, Feinberg must lecture at 10 A.M. But the third condition requires that Jansen's lecture start at some time other than Feinberg's.

D. **Correct.** The following table shows that Guzman can lecture in the library when Kim and Mackey lecture at 9 A.M.:

	8 A.M.	9 A.M.	10 A.M.
Library	Harrison	Kim	Guzman
Studio	Jansen	Mackey	Feinberg

You should be able to verify that this schedule meets all the conditions.

E. **Incorrect.** Assume Harrison lectures in the studio. Harrison's lecture would have to begin at 8 A.M., since Harrison must lecture before Feinberg, who—given that both 9 A.M. slots are filled—must lecture at 10 A.M. Since Jansen must lecture in the studio, Jansen's lecture would have to start at 10 A.M. as well, because that is the only remaining time slot in the studio. This arrangement would violate the third condition.

■ *Difficulty Level: Very difficult*

Question 21 *(page 38)*

Strategy: Try to falsify each response by having Harrison lecture at 9 A.M. with the speaker mentioned in the response lecturing in some place other than that mentioned in the response.

A. **Incorrect.** The following table shows that Feinberg can lecture in the studio even if Harrison lectures at 9 A.M.:

	8 A.M.	9 A.M.	10 A.M.
Library	Guzman	Harrison	Kim
Studio	Jansen	Mackey	Feinberg

You should be able to verify that this schedule meets all the conditions.

B. **Incorrect.** The following table shows that Guzman can lecture in the library even if Harrison lectures at 9 A.M.:

	8 A.M.	9 A.M.	10 A.M.
Library	Guzman	Harrison	Kim
Studio	Jansen	Mackey	Feinberg

You should be able to verify that this schedule meets all the conditions.

C. **Correct.** If Harrison lectures at 9 A.M., Feinberg must lecture at 10 A.M., given that Harrison must start earlier than Feinberg. Given that neither Jansen nor Mackey can start at the same time as Feinberg (third condition), one must start at 8 A.M. and the other at 9 A.M. (in the studio, by the fifth condition). This would leave only the 10 A.M. slot for Harrison were Harrison to lecture in the studio. Thus, Harrison must lecture in the library, if Harrison lectures at 9 A.M.

D. **Incorrect.** The following table shows that Kim can lecture in the library even if Harrison lectures at 9 A.M.:

	8 A.M.	9 A.M.	10 A.M.
Library	Guzman	Harrison	Kim
Studio	Jansen	Mackey	Feinberg

You should be able to verify that this schedule meets all the conditions.

E. **Incorrect.** The following table shows that Mackey can lecture in the studio even if Harrison lectures at 9 A.M.:

	8 A.M.	9 A.M.	10 A.M.
Library	Guzman	Harrison	Kim
Studio	Jansen	Mackey	Feinberg

You should be able to verify that this schedule meets all the conditions.

■ *Difficulty Level: Medium difficulty*

Question 22 (*page 38*)

Strategy: This question is really asking you to determine what *cannot* be true. For each response, try to create an acceptable schedule where the two speakers mentioned start at the same time as each other. If you can't do so for a given response without violating some given condition, then that response is the correct answer.

A. **Incorrect.** Feinberg and Guzman can lecture at the same time as each other, as the following table shows:

	8 A.M.	9 A.M.	10 A.M.
Library	Kim	Harrison	Guzman
Studio	Jansen	Mackey	Feinberg

You should be able to verify that this schedule meets all the conditions. Remember, the second condition merely prevents Feinberg from lecturing earlier than Guzman.

B. **Incorrect.** Feinberg and Kim can lecture at the same time as each other, as the following table shows:

	8 A.M.	9 A.M.	10 A.M.
Library	Guzman	Harrison	Kim
Studio	Jansen	Mackey	Feinberg

You should be able to verify that this schedule meets all the conditions.

C. **Incorrect.** Guzman and Jansen can lecture at the same time as each other, as the following table shows:

	8 A.M.	9 A.M.	10 A.M.
Library	Guzman	Harrison	Kim
Studio	Jansen	Mackey	Feinberg

You should be able to verify that this schedule meets all the conditions.

D. **Correct.** Guzman and Kim cannot lecture at the same time as each other. Since there are three time slots and six speakers, each speaker has to speak at the same time as exactly one other speaker. Feinberg cannot speak at the same time as Harrison (fourth condition), Jansen or Mackey (third condition). This means that Feinberg must lecture at the same time as one of Guzman or Kim, which Feinberg cannot do if Guzman and Kim speak at the same time as each other.

E. **Incorrect.** Guzman and Mackey can speak at the same time as each other, as the following table shows:

	8 A.M.	9 A.M.	10 A.M.
Library	Harrison	Guzman	Kim
Studio	Jansen	Mackey	Feinberg

You should be able to verify that this schedule meets all the conditions.

■ *Difficulty Level: Very difficult*

Question 23 *(page 38)*

Strategy: For each response try to create a schedule with the person mentioned in the response lecturing as stipulated in that response and with Feinberg lecturing in the library at 9 A.M. The only response for which you can do this is the correct answer.

A. **Incorrect.** The second condition requires that Guzman start at 9 A.M. or earlier if Feinberg starts at 9 A.M.

B. **Incorrect.** Harrison must start at 8 A.M., given Feinberg's 9 A.M. start. However, if Harrison lectures in the studio, Jansen and Mackey (not necessarily in that order) would have to start at 9 A.M. and 10 A.M., since the latter two must lecture in the studio, and since those are the only remaining time slots for that room. That means one or the other of Jansen and Mackey would have to lecture at the same time as Feinberg, which would violate the third condition.

C. **Correct.** Assuming Feinberg lectures at 9 A.M., the third condition requires that one of Jansen or Mackey lectures at either 8 A.M., and the other one lectures at 10 A.M. Furthermore, the fifth condition requires both Jansen and Mackey to lecture in the studio. The following table shows that Jansen can lecture in the studio at 10 A.M.:

	8 A.M.	9 A.M.	10 A.M.
Library	Harrison	Feinberg	Kim
Studio	Mackey	Guzman	Jansen

You should be able to verify that this schedule meets all the conditions.

D. **Incorrect.** If Kim lectures in the studio at 9 A.M., Feinberg would have to lecture in the library (at 9 A.M.), and Jansen and Mackey (though not necessarily in that order) would have to lecture in the studio at 8 A.M. and 10 A.M. (given the fifth condition). The fourth condition requires Harrison to lecture at 8 A.M. (since Feinberg lectures at 9 A.M.), and since one of Jansen and Mackey is lecturing at the same time in the studio, Harrison would have to lecture in the library. The only remaining slot for Guzman is 10 A.M. in the library, but the second condition does not permit Feinberg to lecture before Guzman. Thus, Kim cannot lecture in the studio at 9 A.M.

E. **Incorrect.** Given that Feinberg is lecturing at 9 A.M., this response violates the third condition.

■ *Difficulty Level: Difficult*

Question 24 *(page 38)*

Strategy: In each response, you are essentially given half of the schedule of lectures. See if you can complete a full schedule from the partial schedule. If you can, then you have found the correct response.

A. **Incorrect.** Feinberg cannot lecture at 8 A.M., since the fourth condition requires Harrison to lecture earlier than Feinberg.

B. **Incorrect.** This response violates the fifth condition.

C. **Incorrect.** This response violates the fifth condition.

D. **Incorrect.** Harrison cannot lecture at 10 A.M., since the fourth condition requires that Feinberg lecture after Harrison.

E. **Correct.** The following table completes the schedule:

	8 A.M.	9 A.M.	10 A.M.
Library	Harrison	Guzman	Kim
Studio	Mackey	Feinberg	Jansen

You should be able to verify that this schedule meets all the conditions.

■ *Difficulty Level: Difficult*

Serious Tools for ...

Law School Guides

LSACD™ 2001—Computerized Law School Applications and Official Guide to U.S. Law Schools
(Windows-compatible CD-ROM; Web version available via Web site only)
Contains searchable *Official Guide to U.S. Law Schools* and admission applications.
$59

The Official Guide to U.S. Law Schools™ (2001 Edition)
This is the only *official* guide to the 182 American Bar Association (ABA)-approved law schools in the United States, and it's the only one that contains up-to-date admission criteria and other essential admission information provided by the schools themselves. The *Official Guide* is the one book in which each school tells its story so that you can compare and decide which schools are best for you. Tuition, financial aid, special programs, and facilities are only some of the many categories covered in this handy guide.
$19.50

The Whole Law School Package™—TriplePrep Plus & The Official Guide to U.S. Law Schools (2001 Edition)
With this one package you can prepare for the LSAT and find the most accurate and up-to-date information about all 182 ABA-approved law schools. Save money by buying the two books together.
$34

So You Want to Be a Lawyer: A Practical Guide
This newly updated book can save you time and money by showing you how to identify what you should be looking for in a law school, and which ones may be looking for someone like you. Admission office insiders reveal what admission committees look for and how to make your application stand out amid the competition.
$12

Videos

Short Stories From the Real World of Law
A day-in-the-life view of five diverse, working lawyers from across the country. Each profile takes a close-up look at a typical day for a variety of practice areas. Additionally, we get a glimpse of how these particular lawyers balance their personal lives and issues with the dedication and demands of their profession. (20 minutes)
$14

Law School: Achieving the Dream
Law students, professors, and admission professionals talk about the steps you'll need to take to make the dream of law school a reality: preparing for the LSAT, selecting law schools, financing your education, and choosing the school that is right for you. Emphasis is on careful preparation and planning. (20 minutes)
$14

Balancing the Scales: Minorities and Law School
Only one in 25 lawyers in the United States is Asian, Native American, Latino, or African American. Diversity remains an important goal of LSAC-member law schools. This video offers a look at the admission process with a particular focus on the concerns of minority applicants. (20 minutes)
$14

OUTlooks
Law students and admission professionals talk candidly about the issues facing the gay or lesbian law school candidate. Some of the issues addressed include coming out (or not) on your application, identifying schools that are "gay-friendly" and supportive, and the importance of mentors. Several prominent gay attorneys from across the country are profiled as well. (27 minutes)
$14

Indian Lawyers: Translators of Two Worlds
Native American lawyers tell their stories: what inspired them to pursue a law career and the successes and struggles that followed. The stories reflect the ways in which the attorneys forge connections between their cultural values and the law. (20 minutes)
$14

LSAT Preparation

10 Actual, Official LSAT PrepTests

(contains PrepTests 7, 9, 10, 11, 12, 13, 14, 15, 16, 18)
LSAT PrepTests are actual, previously administered LSATs. For pure practice at an unbelievable price, you can't beat 10 *PrepTests* for $29—purchased individually, these 10 practice tests would cost $80. Each test includes an answer key, writing sample, and score-conversion table. (Please note: this book contains *PrepTests* that are also featured in the *Official TriplePreps*.)
$29

LSAT: The Official TriplePrep®—Volume 1

(PrepTests 2, 4, 5)
If you don't have time to take 10 practice tests, you can still save money by purchasing three. Each *Official LSAT TriplePrep* contains three previously administered tests with answer keys, writing samples, and score-conversion tables. *Triple Preps* 1 and 2 also contain 30 additional writing sample prompts for extra practice.
$16.50

LSAT: The Official TriplePrep®—Volume 2

(PrepTests 3, 6, 7)
$16.50

LSAT: The Official TriplePrep®—Volume 3

(PrepTests 8, 9, 10)
$16.50

LSAT: The Official TriplePrep® Plus

(PrepTests 11, 12, 13, explanations, extra writing samples)
TriplePrep Plus provides explanations for all three LSAT-item types. This book also contains 50 previously administered writing sample prompts in addition to three complete PrepTests. (*TriplePrep Plus* is included in *The Whole Law School Package*.)
$18.50

The Official LSAT PrepTest With Explanations™

This new preparation tool includes a previously undisclosed official LSAT (February 1997), with explanations for each and every question in all four multiple-choice sections.
$16.50

The Official LSAT PrepTests®

Each *PrepTest* is an actual LSAT administered on the date indicated. You can practice as if taking an actual test by following the test-taking instructions and timing yourself. In addition to actual LSAT questions, each *PrepTest* contains an answer key, writing sample, and score-conversion table.
$8 each

The Official LSAT PrepTest 19 — June 1996 LSAT
The Official LSAT PrepTest 23 — Oct. 1997 LSAT
The Official LSAT PrepTest 24 — Dec. 1997 LSAT
The Official LSAT PrepTest 25 — June 1998 LSAT
The Official LSAT PrepTest 26 — Sept. 1998 LSAT
The Official LSAT PrepTest 27 — Dec. 1998 LSAT
The Official LSAT PrepTest 28 — June 1999 LSAT
The Official LSAT PrepTest 29 — Oct. 1999 LSAT
The Official LSAT PrepTest 30 — Dec. 1999 LSAT
The Official LSAT PrepTest 31—June 2000 LSAT, *(available late-July 2000)*
The Official LSAT PrepTest 32—Oct. 2000 LSAT, *(available late-Nov. 2000)*
The Official LSAT PrepTest 33—Dec. 2000 LSAT, *(available late-Jan. 2001)*

All prices include postage and handling. Note: Prices and availability of all LSAC products are subject to change. Prices listed in this book are in effect through March 2001. ALL BOOK AND VIDEO SALES ARE FINAL.

Phone
Order by phone 215.968.1001

Online
Order online *www.LSAC.org*

Form
Order on the registration form in the *LSAT/LSDAS Registration and Information Book*